=THE=
SOUTHWESTERN
SAMPLER

Barbara Grunes and Phyllis Magida

CONTEMPORARY
BOOKS, INC.
CHICAGO ▪ NEW YORK

Library of Congress Cataloging-in-Publication Data

Grunes, Barbara.
  The Southwestern sampler.

    1. Cookery, American—Southwestern style.
I. Magida, Phyllis.   II. Title.
TX715.G88   1987   641.5979   87-12303
ISBN 0-8092-4722-4

Published by Contemporary Books, Inc.
180 North Michigan Avenue, Chicago, Illinois 60601
Manufactured in the United States of America
Library of Congress Catalog Card Number: 87-12303
International Standard Book Number: 0-8092-4722-4

Published simultaneously in Canada by Beaverbooks, Ltd.
195 Allstate Parkway, Valleywood Business Park
Markham, Ontario L3R 4T8 Canada

CONTENTS

PREFACE

Just a few years ago, Americans began looking inward for culinary inspiration, rather than outward at France, Italy, China, and Japan, as we had in the past. The result has been not only a greater sense of pride in our national culinary heritage, it has also meant taking a fresh look at our regional cuisines—and at Southwestern cuisine in particular.

We are not Southwesterners: one of us grew up in the East, the other in the Midwest. But we are and have been food professionals for more than 20 years. Instead of considering our outsider status as a disadvantage, we felt it gave us a unique perspective from which to write this cookbook. The knowledgeable outsider often may be able to grasp certain aspects of a cuisine that go unnoticed by a native of the region.

A case in point is the casserole. Casseroles have a special place in Southwestern cooking—at home, in restaurants, in cookbooks and even history books. But no one in the areas we visited or in the homes we were invited to seemed to be aware of it. However, whenever we pointed out the importance of casseroles in the regional cuisine to various Southwestern friends and acquaintances, they heartily agreed with us.

Writing this book gave us an opportunity to study the cuisine in depth, but we were delighted to do so for another reason. Southwestern food is delicious. We knew this long before we started. But we hadn't realized how good the food really was until we began our study. Now we are able to share our discoveries with other food lovers.

We feel that our recipes are up to date, reflecting Southwestern cuisine as it is right now. Our guacamole, for example, is not suggested as an appetizer; we felt that was already old hat. However, it does appear as one of many ingredients in a complex casserole, and we suggest using it as a condiment. Feel free to serve it as an appetizer if you like. We want this to be a "mix-and-match" book to suit your tastes. After all, this is very much what Southwestern cuisine is all about.

INTRODUCTION

This book includes more than 90 recipes for popular Southwestern dishes, some 15 of which are further associated with a particular state, such as Arizona Beef Jerky, Texas Caviar, and New Mexico Sopaipillas.

Also included are special sections on how to construct your own Southwestern cheese tray, how to hold your own chili con carne competition, how to create your own Southwestern casserole, and how to set up your own burrito bar. For quick Southwestern dishes, we refer you to Chapter 11, "Quick and Easy Dishes" (only a list).

We've added yet another special feature that you will not find in any other Southwestern cookbook, one that we're very proud of. We've worked out three chili charts specifying some fresh and dried chilies eaten in each of the three states covered in this cookbook: Arizona, New Mexico, and Texas. We checked with many local authorities—food editors, scientists, etc.—and asked them to name the fresh and dried chilies eaten most frequently in their states. This information is quoted in the copy accompanying each of the three main state chilies: Texas Chili con Carne (Sacred Version), Arizona Chili con Carne, and New Mexico Green Chili Stew. In these charts, we list the chilies, describe them, suggest suitable substitutes, tell you where to get the dried varieties (fresh are too expensive to airfreight if they are not available in your area), indicate the dishes they are used in most frequently, and tell you where to get them in the powdered (and, in the case of the New Mexico chilies, the caribe) form. We think this information will be invaluable when you are planning a really authentic dish.

When we first started on this project, our intention was to present the cuisine while making ourselves as unobtrusive as possible. We soon found out that this is impossible when something as personal as cooking is involved. So, what we're offering here is a Southwestern sampler with a minimum of author-tampering. We have not sifted this wonderful cuisine through the techniques of other cuisines—there is no French green chili *beurre blanc*, for example. Nor will you find that we've recreated the cuisine in our own image. Just as Diego Rivera claimed, "I paint what I see," we have tried to cook only what we found.

But we did want to make a small contribution to the cuisine. We therefore included one special dish that is not strictly authentic, although it is distinctly Southwestern in style. Not finding a Southwestern-style meat loaf in any book or restaurant, we created one, using ground pork, ground beef, chilies, jalapeños, chili powder, onions, garlic, Monterey Jack cheese, and other regional ingredients.

In writing this book, we concentrated on Arizona, Texas, and New Mexico. We excluded California not only because it is a vast state with a varied cuisine all its own, but also because its culinary tendencies are so different from those of the rest of the Southwest.

Please remember that the recipes in this book are just an introduction to a rich, complex, and continually expanding repertoire of dishes. We hope that they will lead you to further explorations of the Southwest's distinctive cuisine. [*Note:* We have used the Spanish spelling of the word *chili* (*chile*) where it appears in Spanish recipe names. Elsewhere, it appears in the common English form, *chili.*]

1
SOUTHWESTERN CUISINE

A Mexican food expert and friend of ours, who had recently returned from a visit to Arizona and Texas, described the food she had encountered there as a sorry American distortion of her beloved Mexican cuisine.

We don't agree with her assessment. To us, Southwestern food is not a border bastard. We see it as a whole cuisine, complete and developed—or rather as complete and developed as any live and evolving cuisine can be.

Of course, you can find the influence of Mexican cuisine in almost any Southwestern dish. Take Chile Relleno Casserole, for example. It originated as a Mexican dish made with fresh peppers stuffed with cheese (or other ingredients), then deep-fried, and topped with a fiery chili sauce. It is still served this way in the Southwest. But Southwesterners have also turned this dish into a casserole, using canned chilies layered with cheese and bottled sauce. In the process, the fresh peppers, the deep-fry, and some of the piquancy were lost. But the cheese content was increased; eggs were added; the flavors, textures, and aromas of the dish were changed; and the shape of the dish was altered. In our opinion, it didn't become a bad chiles rellenos; it became a totally different dish, something belonging to Southwestern, not Mexican, cuisine.

Southwestern cuisine has many special characteristics. Southwesterners have an extraordinary sense of hospitality, for example, inherited from the days when the states were sparsely inhabited territories and conditions were austere.

There's less difference between what the rich and what the poor eat in the Southwest than anywhere else in the country. In the South, for example, the rich eat high off the hog (pork roasts, etc.), while the poor eat low (head cheese, chitlins, etc.). But in the Southwest everybody eats the same sort of food most of the time.

Southwesterners have a sense of humor about their cuisine. Only Southwesterners, for example, hold giant, mock-serious competitions to determine who makes the best bowl of chili. Lately, they've even been holding fajita contests along similar lines. Food contests elsewhere just don't have the same humorous quality. Or take the names of dishes as another example. Border Buttermilk, which is based not on buttermilk but on tequila, implies that what's hard liquor to us is just buttermilk to Southwesterners. Texas Caviar is not caviar at all, but rather giant-size black-eyed peas in vinegar. Consider Kit Carson's last words, which Southwesterners claim were really "Wish I had time for just one more bowl of chili."

Southwestern food has too great a range to be reduced to a few simple rules. Nevertheless, we found nine principles of the cuisine that seem to hold true more often than not.

NINE TENETS OF SOUTHWESTERN CUISINE

1. *Appetizers are essential to the cuisine* and sometimes become the whole meal. "The hearty nature of the region's cooking and its influence from Mexico encourage making whole meals from a selection of appetizers," say authors Dille and Belsinger in *New Southwestern Cooking.* This is certainly true. Appetizers are as important to a Southwesterner as desserts are to an Austrian.
2. *Sauces are served with just about everything savory.* A sauce may be one ingredient in a complex casserole or it may be a casserole topping. It may function as the first layer of a casserole, or it may be spooned over, under, or around a dish. It may be served on the side. But the sauce is always there.
3. *Presentations are always colorful.* The basic hues of the cuisine are red, green, yellow, and blue. Besides the red chilies and sauces and the classic Texas "bowl of red," there are green chilies, green squash, and the classic New Mexico Green Chili Stew. There are the yellows of cheese, corn bread, and tortillas. For the blues, there are blue corn tortillas, blue corn corn bread, and the trendy, brilliant blue margarita.
4. *There's always something to sprinkle on at the table.* Besides the ubiquitous fresh salsa, you'll find as many condiments on a Southwestern table as you will on an East Indian table. These include grated cheese, chopped onion, tomatoes,

lettuce, chilies, olives, green onions, and more. Even Texas and Arizona chilies aren't served without a side of beans, and sometimes rice.

5. *Casseroles are an important culinary form.* Just about everything in the Southwest has been, can be, or will be turned into a casserole. The classic Mexican taco, for example, is often constructed at the table out of refried beans, meat, sour cream, guacamole, chopped onions, red salsa, etc. But in the Southwest, they serve a walking taco, a taco in casserole form with layers of meat, cheese, sauce, chilies, sour cream, and guacamole.

6. *Portions are very large.* Individual servings are so big as to hide the plate. Recipes reflect this tendency, too. Most non-Southwestern recipes yield 4 to 6 servings. But most Southwestern recipes yield 8 to 10, or even 10 to 12, servings.

7. *Tortillas are omnipresent.* Tortillas are the bread of the Southwest, whether they are made of flour or of corn. They are served at all meals and with all courses. They act as the starch layer in a casserole. They serve the purpose of potato chips with dips or of salty nuts and pretzels with drinks. What bread is to a sandwich, the tortilla is to the taco. Tortillas can be used as croutons in salads or as breadcrumbs, if need be.

8. *Chilies are omnipresent.* Whether fresh, dried, flaked, canned, or powdered; whether stuffed, layered, or sprinkled, chilies are found in everything. Southwesterners use them not just for the piquant, hot quality many of them possess, but also for flavor, bulk, and color.

9. *All the above rules are constantly broken.* This is a loose, comfortable, do-anything-you-want kind of cuisine that does not take itself too seriously. If fresh isn't handy, Southwesterners will use something from a can (they used to call cans "airtights"); or they'll use the canned item without bothering to look for the fresh. Ease of preparation and service is constantly stressed in Southwestern cuisine.

2
CHILIES IN VARIOUS FORMS AND HOW TO USE THEM

Not only are there hundreds of varieties of capsicums (chili peppers) to choose from, each with its own taste, texture, heat level, and color, there are also the many forms in which the peppers come, from fresh to powdered, to be considered. To complicate matters further, different chilies are used in different ways in Arizona, New Mexico, and Texas, but these uses will be dealt with in the following chili charts. Chilies appear in one form or another in almost every Southwestern dish (see the Nine Tenets of Southwestern Cuisine in the previous chapter), and the cuisine benefits greatly from their inclusion. Here's a list of the principal forms in which they are found and how to use them:

1. *Fresh.* Many of the larger types of chilies have a skin so tough it should be removed. This is not true of the small, hot green peppers such as jalapeño, which can be used as they come. There are several methods suggested for removing skins from fresh chilies (including roasting them on the grill), but we think the oven broiling method is the most efficient. Lay the chilies close together in a single layer on a cookie sheet lined with aluminum foil. Set the chilies under the broiler and watch them carefully as they will begin to blister quickly. They should be thoroughly blistered in about 3 to 5 minutes. Stay close at hand during the process. At the end of 5 minutes, the skins of the chilies will have loosened and turned black. Put the hot chilies in a plastic bag for 15 minutes. Then slip

the skins off under cold running tap water. Remove the seeds and use as directed in the recipe.

2. *Dried* (large pods). Cover large pods with boiling water and let them soak for an hour in a covered container. Remove pods and discard stems. Hold the softened pods under running water to remove the seeds. Puree the pods in a blender or food processor with some of the chili soaking water. Then put the puree through a strainer to extract any remaining skin. This step takes only a moment and is not at all laborious.

3. *Dried* (small chilies). Break tiny dried chilies in half and shake out the seeds. Break up the chilies as fine as possible and add them to the pot. Or grind them up in a spice mill.

4. *Canned.* Canned hot peppers, such as serrano and jalapeño, are available and their labels accurately indicate what they are. To use, simply drain, cut in half lengthwise, and remove the seeds. Fresh, canned, and brined peppers are interchangeable (although the canned are mellower), unless the recipe specifically calls for, say, a fresh jalapeño. Most canned chilies, however, are marked either mild or hot, chopped or whole, but the variety is not indicated. These are the ones to use when plain chilies are called for. These work just fine in most Southwestern recipes, except in dishes such as chiles rellenos, where the finished product suffers greatly if fresh chilies are not used. To use canned chilies, simply open the can and drain off the liquid.

5. *Frozen.* Chilies are also available frozen, but generally only in the Southwest. Although some shops will airfreight them to you, the cost is prohibitive. If you cannot make the dish without using fresh chilies and you do not live near a source of fresh chilies, we suggest either using canned chilies or making something else. Southwestern cuisine offers dozens of delicious alternatives to dishes requiring fresh or frozen chilies.

6. *Caribe.* All of the New Mexico chili varieties are available in this coarse-flaked form with seeds. (See the New Mexico chili chart.) Although the shops do not specify which chili is being caribed, any of them will work in New Mexico recipes calling for a chili in the caribe form.

7. *Powdered.* Most dried chilies are available in powdered (*molido*) form. This means you can do away with soaking, skinning, and grinding dried chilies to a paste. Powdered chilies are great time and energy savers. If you wish to substitute ancho powder for a large ancho pod, for example, simply buy the ancho powder and use 1 tablespoon of powder for every dried ancho the recipe calls for. To make an Arizona Chili con Carne using powder, for example, simply measure 6 tablespoons dried Anaheim chili powder and 6 tablespoons dried pasilla powder

into a blender. Add $\frac{1}{2}$ teaspoon dried tepin powder for each tepin chili you would have included. Add a small amount of water and mix to a paste. Add this paste to the chili con carne just as you would have added a paste made from dried, soaked chilies. In fact, you will not be able to tell the difference. Please note that in using powdered chilies, you will lose some flavor and piquancy. The older the powder is, the more you will lose. Nevertheless, many cooks feel that the time saved more than compensates for the loss of flavor. This is entirely up to you. Numerous Southwestern cooks use the powders, which is why they are so widely available. See the chili charts of individual states or the appendix for mail-order sources for the powders. In this book we refer to all powdered dried chilies as pure ground chili powders to differentiate them from commercial chili powder.

8. *Commercial chili powder.* This item is a blend of a pure ground chili powder, such as ancho or New Mexico #6, and other spices, such as garlic powder, cumin, and oregano. Commercial chili powder, while it has its place, is not even remotely interchangeable with the pure ground chili powders. For information on where to send for a couple of the Texas-style commercial chili powders, see the Texas chili chart.

TAKE CARE IN HANDLING HOT CHILIES

Use care in handling hot chilies. They contain capsaicin, the source of the heat in the chili. Some chilies are so hot that they cause actual burning sensations. To be on the safe side, observe the following precautions:

1. Use rubber gloves when handling hot peppers, even the canned variety.
2. Never touch the sensitive area around your eyes after working with hot peppers. Avoid direct contact with skin.
3. Wash your hands well after handling hot peppers.
4. If you use a food processor or a blender to grind the hot peppers, open the lid away from you and don't breathe in the vapors directly.

ARIZONA CHILIES	DESCRIPTION	FUNCTION & HEAT LEVEL	WHERE AVAILABLE	WHERE AVAILABLE POWDERED
Anaheim (dried)	Red pod	Color and bulk; mild to medium hot	South Texas Spice Co.	Substitute California powdered at Reynoso Bros.
Anaheim (fresh)	5″ to 8″ long; 1½″ to 2″ wide; bright green, tapers to point	Bulk and heat; mild to medium hot		
Jalapeño (fresh)	2″ long; 1″ wide; dark green	Heat; hot/hot	May substitute canned, available in supermarkets	
Pasilla (dried)	Long slender dried pod with blackish color	Bulk and heat; mild to hot	La Preferida Bolner's	Reynoso Bros.
Serrano (fresh)	1½″ long; ⅜″ wide; medium green, pointed end	Heat; hot/hot		
Tepin (dried)	Tiny round dried red pepper	Heat and flavoring; hot	Morgans Reynoso Bros.	
Yellow Way (fresh)	1½″ to 2″ long; 1″ wide; yellow	Heat; hot		

NEW MEXICO CHILIES	DESCRIPTION	FUNCTION & HEAT LEVEL	WHERE AVAILABLE	WHERE AVAILABLE POWDERED
Big Jim Numex (dried)	Red	Bulk and color; mild to mildly hot		Mexican Connection (powdered and caribe)
Big Jim Numex (fresh)	7″ long; 1½″ to 2″ wide; medium bright green	Bulk and color; mild to mildly hot		
Española Improved (dried)	Bright red	Bulk, color, and heat; hot to very hot	Buenos Foods	Buenos Foods Mexican Connection (powdered and caribe)
Española Improved (fresh)	4″ long; 1½″ wide; medium dark green	Bulk, color, and heat; hot to very hot		
Jalapeño (fresh)	2″ long; 1″ wide; dark green	Heat; hot/hot	May substitute canned, available in supermarkets	
New Mexico #6 (dried)	Red	Bulk and color; mildly hot	Casados Farms Bolner's Mexican Connection	Casados Farms Mexican Connection (powdered and caribe)
New Mexico #6 (fresh)	4″ to 8″ long; 1½″ to 2″ wide; bright green, pointed tip	Bulk and color; mildly hot		

NEW MEXICO CHILIES	DESCRIPTION	FUNCTION & HEAT LEVEL	WHERE AVAILABLE	WHERE AVAILABLE POWDERED
Scandia A (dried)	Red	Bulk, color, and heat; hot to very hot	Buenos Foods	Buenos Foods Mexican Connection (powdered and caribe)
Scandia A (fresh)	7" long; 1½" to 2" wide; medium bright green	Bulk, color, and heat; hot to very hot		

TEXAS CHILIES	DESCRIPTION	FUNCTION & HEAT LEVEL	WHERE AVAILABLE	WHERE AVAILABLE POWDERED
Ancho (dried)	5" long; 3" wide; triangular, deep maroon to black	Bulk and color; mild to medium hot	La Preferida Bolner's South Texas Spice Co.	La Preferida
Ancho (fresh)	4" to 5" long; 3" wide; glossy mahagony	Bulk and color; mild to medium hot		
Arbol (dried)	Red, long, and thin	Very hot	Bolner's La Preferida	Reynoso Bros.
Cascabel (dried)	¾" to 1½" diameter; dark reddish brown	Color and heat; moderately hot to hot	Bolner's Reynoso Bros. South Texas Spice Co.	
Fiesta Brand Fancy Light Chili Powder				Bolner's
Gebhardt Eagle Brand Chili Powder			The Gebhardt Co. was not able to locate a source for their product by mail	
Jalapeño (fresh)	2" long; 1" wide; dark green	Heat; hot/hot	May substitute canned, available in supermarkets	
Japones (also Jap) (dried)	Mahogany to red	Hot	Bolner's La Preferida South Texas Spice Co.	
New Mexico #6 (dried)	Red	Bulk and color; mildly hot	Casados Farms Bolner's Mexican Connection	Casados Farms Mexican Connection Powdered and Caribe
Pasilla (dried)	Long slender dried pod with blackish color	Bulk and heat; mild to hot	La Preferida Bolner's	Reynoso Bros.
Pequines (dried)	¼" long; oval	Very hot	Bolner's South Texas Spice Co. Mexican Connection	

TEXAS CHILIES	DESCRIPTION	FUNCTION & HEAT LEVEL	WHERE AVAILABLE	WHERE AVAILABLE POWDERED
Petines (dried)	¼″ diameter; round or oval	Very hot	Bolner's South Texas Spice Co.	
Serrano (fresh)	1½″ long; ⅜″ wide; medium green, pointed end	Heat; hot/hot		

3
DRINKS
AND
APPETIZERS

HOW TO DRINK TEQUILA (OR TECATE)

We suggest serving margaritas with our cheese tray. But in case anyone wants to drink Tecate beer, or in case some spirited tequila drinker wants his tequila straight, we're including directions for both tequila and Tecate beer drinking. Both of these have their own drinking ritual, which originated in Mexico but then spread to the border.

Tequila, salt, and lime seem to have a natural affinity for each other. A knowledgeable, hard-core tequila drinker will go through the following steps before he takes his first sip of tequila. First, he licks the soft saddle of his left hand with his tongue (the soft saddle is the area between the thumb and index finger). He then sprinkles this area with salt. Some tequila drinkers now squeeze a few drops of lime onto the salt. The tequila buff now takes a lick of salt, followed promptly by a slug of tequila. Another method is to dip a wedge of lime in salt and alternate between sucks of salted lime and sips of tequila.

The Tecate beer-drinking ritual is similar to the tequila ritual: simply remove the flip top off a well-chilled can of Tecate (or substitute your favorite brand of Mexican beer). Shake some salt on the top of the can (not in the hole) and squeeze a few drops of lime onto the salt. Sip the beer, taking care to incorporate some salt and lime into each sip.

And now for the perfect margarita.

THE PERFECT MARGARITA

$\frac{1}{2}$ **lime, sliced**

2 **large champagne glasses, the old-fashioned, wide-mouth type (or substitute 2 balloon wine glasses)**

Dish filled $\frac{1}{4}$-inch deep with coarse salt

12 **ice cubes or 2 very large handfuls crushed ice**

$\frac{1}{4}$ **cup fresh, strained lime juice**

$\frac{1}{4}$ **cup triple sec**

$\frac{1}{4}$ **cup confectioners' sugar**

$\frac{3}{4}$ **cup good-quality tequila**

2 **thin slices lime, for garnish**

1. Run lime slices around the rim of each glass, then invert and dip in coarse salt. The salt will stick to the wet area. Turn the glasses right side up and place them in the freezer so that they will frost when you return them to room temperature.

2. Process the ice cubes in a food processor or blender to make crushed ice.

3. Pour the lime juice, triple sec, confectioners' sugar, and tequila over the ice. Process again for a few seconds until well mixed.

4. Remove the glasses from the freezer and carefully transfer the margarita mixture to them, taking care not to disturb the ice. Arrange a lime slice on each glass so that it straddles the rim.

Makes 2 double servings

BLUE MARGARITA

To make the trendy blue margarita, simply substitute $\frac{1}{4}$ cup blue curaçao for the triple sec. The drink will taste the same (both triple sec and curaçao are orange liqueurs), but the margarita will now be a brilliant blue. Blue curaçao gets its color from pure food coloring.

SOUTHWESTERN CHEESE TRAY

You don't need Brie and Gorgonzola to put together a sophisticated cheese tray for a small cocktail party. Simply assemble some of the cheeses (five is a good number) frequently eaten in the Southwest. Add some homemade tortilla chips, some margaritas, a jar of homemade jalapeño jelly (see Index), and a fondue pot full of Chile con Queso (see Index). You don't need pears for palate cleansers either. Simply put out some jicama cut into matchsticks. Jicama, a root vegetable indigenous to the Southwest, has an applelike flavor with a suggestion of pineapple and a texture and mouth feel similar to those of a raw potato. (In big cities, jicama is available in Mexican groceries).

For the cheese tray, you will need:

1. *Five cheeses.* These should include a Longhorn cheddar and a Monterey Jack, both of which are prominent in Southwestern cuisine. The remaining three should be Mexican-style cheeses, one from each of the following categories if possible: Fresco Queso, a fresh, pure white cheese with a salty, tangy flavor and a crumbly texture; Queso Chihuahua, a creamy white, mild cheese, similar to a mild cheddar and named after Chihuahua, Mexico, where it was created (if possible, get a Chihuahua with jalapeño peppers added); and Queso Anejo, an aged, creamy white cheese the same color as Chihuahua, but with a drier texture and a sharper, saltier flavor. (If Queso Anejo is not available—and it is hard to get in some markets—a good substitute might be a Spanish import called El Campillo.)

   A cheese tray is most effective visually when each cheese is a different shape and color. You might include a large wedge or round piece of Longhorn cheddar, a block of Monterey Jack, and different presentations for each of the Mexican cheeses, e.g., a whole round cheese, a wedge lying on its side, a half of a round cheese, etc.

2. *Jicama sticks.* If possible, arrange the jicama in the center of the cheese tray. If there is no room, serve the jicama on a separate tray. You will need one jicama root, two limes cut into wedges, and a tiny bowl of pure ground (hot, if desired) chili powder. Peel the jicama and cut it into $1/2$-inch matchsticks. Arrange these around the small bowl of chili powder and the lime wedges. To eat, squeeze a lime wedge over a jicama stick, then dip it into chili powder.

3. *Tortillas and tortilla chips.* You will want to set out two side dishes, one of warmed flour tortillas and the other of homemade tortilla chips, to go with the cheeses.

4. *Chile con Queso.* This melted cheese fondue with chilies is set near the tortillas and tortilla chips as a dip. A tiny side dish filled with finely chopped, seeded jalapeño peppers (the canned have a mellower flavor) may also be set out for guests to sprinkle on their fondue.

5. *A log of cream cheese topped with sweet and hot Jalapeño–Red Pepper Jelly* (see Index). Form an 8-ounce block of cream cheese into a thin, 8-inch-long log. Set this in the middle of a serving platter, spoon jelly over it to cover completely, and surround it with homemade tortilla chips. Southwesterners also serve crackers with this delicacy.

6. *A tray full of margaritas* (see Index). Or substitute the exciting Blue Margaritas (see Index) and Tecate or any Mexican beer. Be sure to set out two small dishes, one filled with salt and the other with lime wedges if you are serving Mexican beer.

CHILE CON QUESO

2 tablespoons vegetable oil
1 medium onion, minced
1 4-ounce can chopped green chilies, drained
$\frac{1}{2}$ teaspoon each salt and chili caribe flakes
8 ounces sharp cheddar, shredded
8 ounces Monterey Jack, shredded
1 5-ounce can evaporated milk
Tortilla chips

1. Heat the vegetable oil in a large, heavy skillet or fondue pot. Sauté the onion until tender. Stir in the chilies, salt, and chili caribe flakes, and continue cooking until liquid has evaporated, about 3 to 4 minutes, stirring often.

2. Reduce heat to low. Sprinkle in the cheeses and blend in evaporated milk. Stir until cheese has melted. Serve hot in the skillet or fondue pot. Serve with warm tortilla chips.

Makes 6 to 8 servings

JALAPEÑO PEPPER JELLY

Jalapeño jelly is a vibrant green, sweet, yet tangy-tasting jelly. Try it on crackers with cheese. We hesitate to use food coloring, but in this case we like the crisp color it adds. If you do not choose to use it the jelly will have a slightly lighter color but it will taste just as good.

> 1 large red bell pepper, seeded, deveined, and chopped
> 6 fresh jalapeño peppers, seeded, deveined, and chopped
> 6 cups sugar
> $1^1/_2$ cups cider vinegar
> 2 drops green food coloring (optional)
> 1 6-ounce twin-pack Certo

1. Place the peppers in a heavy saucepan. Stir in the sugar and cider vinegar. Bring the mixture to a boil over medium heat. Continue boiling for 45 seconds to 1 minute. Blend in the food coloring, if desired, and add Certo.

2. Ladle jelly into sterilized jelly jars. Cool.

3. Stir three or four times during the cooling process to keep the peppers evenly distributed.

4. Seal the jars according to package directions.

Makes 8 6-ounce jelly jars

HOMEMADE TORTILLA CHIPS

3 7-inch flour tortillas
Vegetable oil for deep-frying
Salt

1. Cut each tortilla into wedge-shaped quarters.

2. Heat oil to 375°F on frying thermometer. Slide tortilla quarters into deep, hot fat; let them cook until they are crisp and brown. Remove chips from fat with a slotted spoon and drain on paper towels. Sprinkle with salt.

Makes 12

MINIATURE TORTILLA BASKETS

Little, deep-fried tortilla baskets are easily made by cutting 2½-inch circles out of the tortillas with a cookie cutter, then pressing each circle into the shape of a little basket between two little strainers, such as tea strainers. The strainers should then be immersed in 375°F fat and the tortillas cooked until crisp or golden brown. Fill the baskets with guacamole to garnish a salad, or serve with chips, or with refried beans to garnish a steak-type dish. They can even be used as individual condiment baskets, filled with salsa, sour cream, grated cheese, chopped olives, etc. Baskets can be made larger, using two large strainers or a potato basket fryer. (See index for Large Tortilla Baskets.)

CREAMY BEAN DIP

   3 tablespoons bacon drippings
   3 cups Refried Beans (see Index)
   ½ teaspoon each chili caribe flakes, ground cumin, and salt
   ¼ teaspoon pepper
   1 cup sour cream
   Flour or corn tortilla chips, or both

   1. Heat drippings in a heavy skillet. Stir in the refried beans. Season with chili caribe flakes, ground cumin, salt, and pepper.
   2. When the beans have reached the desired thickness, place them in a serving dish or tortilla basket and stir in the sour cream.
   3. Serve at room temperature with tortilla chips, homemade or commercial.

Makes 6 servings

TEXAS CAVIAR

Texans serve this recipe on January 1 because of an old Southern custom that holds that anyone who eats black-eyed peas on New Year's Day will prosper throughout the year. Texans, however, have made this dish more Southwestern than Southern, not only by giving it a Texan monicker, but also by adding the tongue-in-cheek "caviar" to the name of the recipe. Texans have changed the preparation as well. Southern black-eyed peas are often served plain. Or they may be simmered with bacon and molasses or red pepper. But in Texas, the "caviar" is marinated in vinegar, onions, and garlic. Most Texas Caviar recipes call for one onion to this quantity of beans; but so many guests requested extra onion when we test-served this dish, that we changed the amount to two onions.

2 cups dried black-eyed peas
Water to cover
2 garlic cloves, peeled and mashed
2 onions, cut in paper-thin slices, then separated into rings
³/₄ cup wine vinegar
1 cup vegetable oil
2 teaspoons salt
1 teaspoon freshly ground black pepper

1. Place the black-eyed peas in a large pot and pick them over carefully, discarding any that may be discolored or unhealthy-looking. Cover with water and leave overnight. The peas should absorb the water, soften, and swell to a 5-cup volume by the next day.

2. Drain the peas, place them in a saucepan, cover them with fresh water, and simmer them until tender, about 1 hour. Drain the peas and place them in a ceramic or earthenware dish. Do not use metal—the peas are going to marinate in vinegar.

3. Place the garlic in a small saucepan along with the onions and wine vinegar. Bring to a boil and immediately remove from heat. Stir in the oil, salt, and pepper, and pour this mixture over the peas.

4. Allow to cool, cover (do not use aluminum foil), and refrigerate for at least 24 hours. This dish is better if it is allowed to marinate for two or even three days. Serve as an appetizer or side dish alone, or with warmed tortillas, if desired.

Makes 5 cups

CHILI-PEANUT POPCORN

6 tablespoons butter
1 teaspoon Gebhardt Eagle Brand or Fiesta Brand Fancy Light
chili powder
1 teaspoon garlic powder
$\frac{1}{2}$ pound unsalted, roasted peanuts
2 quarts freshly popped popcorn

1. Melt the butter over medium heat in a small saucepan. Stir in the chili powder, garlic powder, and peanuts. Continue cooking for 3 minutes, stirring often.

2. Place the popcorn in a large bowl. Toss with the hot butter mixture. Serve immediately.

Makes 2 quarts

BLUE CORN NACHOS

1 8-ounce package blue corn chips
8 ounces Monterey Jack or Longhorn cheddar, grated
$\frac{1}{4}$ cup fresh jalapeño peppers, seeded, deveined, and sliced thin
(canned are acceptable)

1. Arrange the blue corn chips in an ovenproof dish and sprinkle them with grated cheese.

2. Place the dish under a preheated broiler, on the middle rack, for 1 minute, or until the cheese has melted. Check the cheese often because it melts fast.

3. Remove the nachos from the oven, sprinkle with peppers, and serve hot.

Makes 6 to 8 servings

NACHO FRIES IN A BASKET

Traditional nachos are made of tortilla chips (preferably homemade), strewn in a single layer on a cookie sheet, liberally covered with grated Monterey Jack, broiled until the cheese melts, and sprinkled with chopped jalapeños. But the simplicity of their preparation is in inverse proportion to their popularity. In fact, nacho chips are so popular an appetizer in the Southwest that if we were a bowl of salted peanuts, we'd be looking nervously over our shoulders. The popularity of nachos has encouraged the development of numerous toppings, including shredded chicken, refried beans, guacamole and sour cream, black olives, and red enchilada sauce. This, a Nacho Fries variant, was so delicious we recreated it for this book after finding it served in a restaurant.

> **4 flour Large Tortilla Baskets (see Index)**
> **Oil for deep-frying**
> **4 large Idaho potatoes**
> **1 pound Monterey Jack or Longhorn cheddar, grated**
> **1 12-ounce can evaporated milk**
> **8 fresh or canned jalapeño peppers, seeded and cut into thin**
>   **widthwise slices**

1. Prepare the flour Large Tortilla Baskets. Baskets may be prepared up to a week ahead of time if, after frying, they are stored in airtight containers. When you are ready to use them, right before frying the potatoes, remove the baskets from their containers and place each one in a small bowl.

2. Peel the potatoes and cut them into thin widthwise strips. Place the potatoes in a bowlful of cold water until you are ready to deep-fry. Fill your largest kettle half full of vegetable oil and heat it to 375°F on a deep-fat thermometer.

4. Drain the potatoes and dry them carefully on kitchen towels. Drop the potatoes, a few at a time, into the hot fat. Let them fry until crisp and brown.

5. Meanwhile, put the cheese and evaporated milk in the top of a double boiler set over boiling water, and stir often until the cheese melts.

6. When the potatoes are crisp and brown, remove them from the hot oil, using a slotted spoon, and drain them on paper towels. Quickly divide the potatoes among the fried tortilla baskets, arranging the potatoes so they are standing up.

7. Quickly divide the melted cheese among the four nests. Then sprinkle chopped jalapeños over the cheese. Serve immediately.

Makes 4 servings

RIBS WITH BARBECUE SAUCE

Ribs in the Southwest are always cooked in a Texas-style pit or smoker, or on the grill. For cooks with only an oven, here is another way to go.

3–4 pounds pork baby back ribs
Water to cover
$^1/_2$ **teaspoon freshly ground pepper**
1 medium onion, sliced
2 bay leaves
$^1/_4$ **teaspoon salt**

1. With a sharp knife cut between the ribs to separate. Place the ribs and the remaining ingredients in a large, heavy saucepan. Bring to a boil and reduce the heat to a simmer. Continue cooking for 15 minutes. Drain ribs. Arrange the ribs in a 9″ × 13″ baking pan or on a cookie sheet lined with aluminum foil.

2. Brush the ribs with sauce and bake in a preheated 350°F oven for 1 hour. Turn the ribs every 20 minutes and baste with sauce until coated. Or grill complete slabs over ashen coals of charcoal, mesquite, or hickory chips, or a combination of woods.

3. Serve hot. Pass extra sauce at the table.

Serves 10 as an appetizer

BARBECUE SAUCE

3 tablespoons vegetable oil
1 medium onion, minced
3 cloves garlic, minced
1 cup catsup
1 cup chili sauce
4 tablespoons cider vinegar
3 tablespoons dark brown sugar
1 teaspoon dry mustard
2 teaspoons Gebhardt Eagle Brand or Fiesta Brand Fancy Light
   chili powder

Whisk all ingredients together in a saucepan. Bring mixture to a boil over medium heat. Reduce heat to a simmer and continue cooking for 5 minutes, stirring often. Cool sauce. Place in a covered container and refrigerate until ready to serve. If a thinner sauce is desired, blend in a small amount of water or tomato sauce.

Makes 1¾ cups sauce

SOUTHWESTERN PIZZA

Oil for deep-frying
2 10-inch flour tortillas
2 tablespoons vegetable oil
1 red bell pepper, seeded and cut into rings
1 large onion, chopped fine
1 large clove garlic, chopped fine
1 cup canned refried beans
2 cups (or more) Red Enchilada Sauce (see Index) or use a good commercial substitute
1 pound Homemade Mock Chorizo, cooked and drained according to method 2 (see Index)
1 pound Monterey Jack or Longhorn cheddar, grated
1–2 canned jalapeño peppers, seeded and chopped fine

1. Heat oil to 375°F. Fry tortillas, one at a time, until golden and crisp. Drain on paper towels.

2. Meanwhile, heat 2 tablespoons oil in a separate skillet. Sauté bell pepper, onion, and garlic for about 5 minutes, or until onions are limp.

3. Spread each tortilla with ½ cup refried beans. Divide the onion mixture between the two pizzas and sprinkle equal amounts on each.

4. Spoon 1 cup (or more) Red Enchilada Sauce over each pizza, covering the beans as well as possible, but not too heavily.

5. Divide the Homemade Mock Chorizo (well drained in a colander) into two equal parts and sprinkle it over the sauce on each pizza.

6. Sprinkle half the cheese (8 ounces) on each pizza. Then scatter finely chopped jalapeños over each pizza.

7. Bake in a 350°F oven for about 15 minutes, or until the cheese has melted and the pizzas are heated through. Serve immediately.

Makes 3 to 4 servings

GRINGO TOSTADAS

1 **cup vegetable oil**
6 **flour tortillas**
1 **recipe Fast Refried Beans (see Index)**
1 **small head lettuce, shredded**
2 **large tomatoes, chopped**
2 **cups sharp Longhorn cheddar, shredded**
$\frac{1}{4}$ **cup fresh jalapeño peppers, seeded, deveined, and chopped
    (canned are acceptable)**

1. Heat $\frac{1}{4}$ inch oil in a heavy skillet to 375°F. Slip a tortilla into the hot oil and fry it on both sides for about 30 seconds, using tongs to turn it. When it is a light golden brown, remove it from the oil and drain it on paper towels. Repeat with the remaining tortillas. If necessary, keep the tortillas warm by wrapping them in aluminum foil or placing them in a preheated 250°F oven.

2. When you are ready to serve, place the warm tortillas on a serving dish. Divide the remaining ingredients and place them in order on each tortilla. Tortillas are best when they are served fresh and hot.

Makes 6 servings

4

CHILIES: CON CARNE AND SIN CARNE

TEXAS CHILI CON CARNE
(SACRED VERSION)

What makes a bowl of Texas Chili con Carne classic? And what chili peppers should be used in it? Research indicated that Texas chili has evolved into two separate versions: a sacred version, made according to well-established rules; and a secular, popular version that is commonly made throughout Texas today. We decided to synthesize our findings and devise some guidelines that would allow anyone to produce either version. We consulted many sources, among them H. Allen Smith's *A Bowl of Red* and a book from the Time-Life Foods of the World series called *American Cooking: The Great West*, whose author Jonathan Norton Leonard was assisted by the late James Beard as consultant.

Here are some rules to help you make the classic Texas chili:

Nine Rules for Texas Chili con Carne
(Sacred Version)

1. The main ingredient of the sacred version of Texas Chili con Carne is lean venison or beef, which is never ground, but cut into bite-size, $1/2$-inch cubes.
2. The meat must always be browned in rendered beef suet, not oil or butter. (Ask your butcher to grind the suet so that it liquefies quickly.)

3. Use three Texas chili pods for each pound of meat and as many chili peppers (the small, hot variety) as you want. But make sure that some of the chilies are of the ancho variety, since these are the reddest of all and will add color to your "bowl of red." (See the section below for appropriate pods and peppers).
4. Use only a little garlic. We interpret this to mean about half a clove per pound of meat. If you feel that "only a little" means a small clove per pound of meat, by all means go ahead and use that amount.
5. Use only the liquid in which the chili peppers soak as chili water. To make sure your water is sufficient, we suggest using 10 cups of water to soak the nine pods needed for each 3 pounds of meat. The meat will not be tender enough unless it is first boiled in the right amount of chili water, before the chili pulp is added.
6. Use only a little oregano and cumin. We interpret this to mean 1 teaspoon of each for each 3 pounds of meat.
7. Use absolutely no tomatoes, onions, or beans.
8. Classic Texas Chili con Carne is not very liquid. If thickening is needed, use cornmeal or masa harina, not cornstarch or flour.
9. Classic Texas Chili con Carne is often served with two side dishes—one of rice, one of pinto beans. The pinto beans served with Texas chili are whole. The beans served as a side dish with Arizona chili are refried.

What Texas Chilies to Use

"The fresh chilies Texans most often use are jalapeños, fresh anchos, and serranos," says Candy Sagon, food editor for the *Dallas Times Herald Morning News*. "But they don't put these in their chili con carne; they save the fresh chilies for the salsas. Texans don't use fresh chilies in their chili con carne because we don't like those little bits of green floating about. Also, we prefer a more unified heat, not the occasional hot mouthful you get when using fresh chilies."

Sagon explains that the use of dried chilies requires the cook to make a chili water, which allows the heat to be controlled—the more chili water you add, the hotter the chili con carne will be. "Besides this," she adds, "dried chili peppers are red. And this is what we're making—a bowl of red.

"Today," she continues, "most Texans use commercial chili powder in their chili con carne; or they use a combination of dried chilies and commercial chili powder. A few use just dried chilies, but these are not in the majority."

We asked Michael Bolner, sales manager of a family-owned business called Bolner's Fiesta Products in San Antonio, what dried chilies were most commonly used in Texas Chili con Carne. Bolner, who is one of the largest suppliers of dried chili peppers and pods (pods are the larger, meaty chilies), said that the four dried pods most often used in Texas Chili con Carne were dried ancho, New Mexico #6 dried, dried pasilla, and dried cascabel. "The pods add flavor to the chili con carne," he says. "But it's the small peppers that add heat. Peppers most commonly used in Texas Chili con Carne include petines, pequines, arbol chilies, a chili marketed as Chinese chili, and a group of peppers that used to come from the Orient and that are marketed as jap peppers." (Jap pepper is common usage and will be used throughout this book. These peppers are formally referred to as japones peppers.)

TEXAS CHILI CON CARNE
(SACRED VERSION)

Venison is spectacular in this dish. It can be mail-ordered from Wild Game, Inc. See the Appendix for mail-order sources.

3 dried ancho chili pods

6 dried chili pods, any one or combination of the following: New Mexico #6, pasilla, or cascabel

9 dried chili peppers, any one or combination of the following: petines, pequines, arbol, Chinese chilies, or jap peppers

10 cups boiling water

6 ounces beef suet

3 pounds very lean venison or beef round, cut into ½-inch cubes

1½ cloves garlic

1 teaspoon each oregano and cumin

Salt to taste

Cornmeal or masa harina (optional)

Side dishes of pinto beans and rice

1. First, soak the peppers in boiling water so that there will be chili water in which to simmer the meat. Put the three ancho and the other six pods in a large pot and cover with 9 cups boiling water. Cover the pan and let soak for 1 hour.

2. Tear the nine tiny dried chili peppers of your choice in half and shake them to extract and discard the seeds. Put these chilies in a second bowl and cover with 1 cup boiling water. Let soak for 1 hour.

3. While the chilies soak, render the beef suet. Place the suet in a small, heavy-bottomed saucepan over medium heat and let it melt. Watch it carefully, stirring occasionally. As soon as it is rendered, remove it from heat and strain. Measure out ¼ cup and reserve. Then pour the remainder into a small glass jar with a lid and refrigerate or freeze it for later use. Incidentally, some people love the taste of the remaining suet bits.

4. When the chili pods and peppers have soaked for 1 hour, strain them both and combine the liquids. Immediately heat the reserved suet in a deep, heavy-bottomed soup kettle or a very large frying pan. Brown the cubes of meat slowly on all sides, using a wooden spoon to turn the meat. When the meat is browned, pour in 5 cups of reserved chili water, bring to a boil, reduce the heat to a simmer, and cook for 40 to 60 minutes, or until the meat is tender. This may take up to 2 hours.

5. While the meat is cooking, prepare the chili pulp. Hold each pod under running tap water to extract the seeds. Discard stems. Traditionally, the next step is to rub the chili pods through a strainer to get rid of skins—a laborious and time-consuming process. We suggest pureeing the pods in a blender or food processor before rubbing them through a strainer. Done this way, the strainer step takes only a minute.

6. When the meat is tender, cut or tear the tiny chili peppers into small pieces and add them to the pot. Then stir in the strained chili pod pulp. Add additional chili soaking water, as needed either for liquid or for taste.

7. Stir in the garlic, oregano, cumin, and salt. Simmer 15 more minutes, then check consistency. If the chili is too liquid, add cornmeal or masa harina, one tablespoon at a time, simmering for a few minutes after each addition, until the desired consistency is reached. Taste for salt, adding more if desired.

8. Serve with side dishes of pinto beans and rice.

Makes 8 to 10 servings

TEXAS CHILI CON CARNE
(SECULAR VERSION)

Texas Chili con Carne (secular version) has a bad reputation. Although purists may not like the coarse grind of the meat, the omission of the beef suet, the inclusion of tomatoes and onions, the commercial chili powder, and the beans, we maintain (along with most of America) that chili con carne doesn't have to conform to the classic version's standards to be delicious. We're including here two recipes for secular chili con carne, one of them the recipe which President Lyndon B. Johnson and Mrs. Ladybird Johnson contributed to the genre.

Commercial Texas chili powder, the kind used in secular chili con carne, is usually based on one type of mild chili. The popular Texas chili powder, called Fiesta Brand Fancy Light chili powder, uses mainly ancho chilies. Another popular Texas brand, called Gebhardt Eagle Brand chili powder, uses the New Mexico #6 chili, similar to and also known as the California Anaheim. The reason commercial chili powders are frowned on by purists is because, along with the ground chilies, they include such spices as cumin, oregano, garlic (or garlic powder), and salt.

TEXAS CHILI CON CARNE
(SECULAR VERSION)

3 tablespoons vegetable oil

4 cloves garlic, minced fine

2 medium onions, chopped coarse

2 pounds coarsely ground round steak

6 cups water

1 28-ounce can tomatoes, with their liquid

$\frac{1}{2}$ cup commercial Texas chili powder

2 teaspoons oregano

$1\frac{1}{2}$ teaspoons each cumin and salt

1 teaspoon cayenne pepper, or to taste

$\frac{1}{2}$ teaspoon sugar

1 16-ounce can red kidney beans, drained
1–2 tablespoons yellow cornmeal (optional)
Oyster crackers (optional)

1. Heat the oil in a large skillet. Cook the garlic and onions until the onion is limp. Add the beef, breaking it up well with a wooden spoon, and brown on all sides.

2. Add water and canned tomatoes with their liquid, breaking up each one with your hands.

3. Add commercial chili powder, oregano, cumin, salt, cayenne pepper, and sugar, stirring well to combine.

4. Simmer the chili con carne for 1 hour, uncovered, adding more water as needed. Stir in the beans and heat for 5 minutes.

5. Check the consistency and taste for salt. The secular version of chili con carne is soupier than the classic. But if it is too soupy, either continue cooking it until some of the liquid evaporates or add some cornmeal to thicken it. Serve immediately. Some people add oyster crackers to secular chili con carne.

Makes 4 to 6 servings

LBJ'S PEDERNALES RIVER CHILI

Chili meat is coarsely ground round steak or well-trimmed chuck. The following recipe calls for the meat to be coarse ground on a ¾ plate. This is the standard secular chili grind, but it is increasingly difficult to obtain because it is dangerous for butchers to work with such a large grinding hole. Nevertheless, even a ¼-inch grind gives a satisfyingly meaty chew to chili meat. For the following recipe, we suggest adding 1½ teaspoons salt and doubling the amount of commercial chili powder to 12 teaspoons (4 tablespoons). Here's the LBJ recipe exactly as it appeared in newspapers all over the country during his presidency.

4 pounds chili meat
1 large onion, chopped
2 cloves garlic
1 teaspoon ground oregano
1 teaspoon cumin seed
6 teaspoons chili powder, or to taste
1½ cups canned whole tomatoes
2–6 generous dashes liquid hot sauce
Salt to taste
2 cups hot water

1. Place the meat, onion, and garlic in a large, heavy frying pan or dutch oven. Cook until light in color.

2. Add oregano, cumin seed, chili powder, tomatoes, hot sauce, salt, and hot water. Bring to a boil, lower heat, and simmer about 1 hour. Skim off fat during cooking.

Makes 8 to 12 servings

NEW MEXICO GREEN CHILI STEW

Ask for a bowl of chili almost anywhere in New Mexico and you'll be asked this three-word question: "Red or green?" "Red" refers to Texas Chili con Carne, either secular or classic. "Green" means either of two dishes: a green chili stew made with any variety of fresh New Mexico chili peppers, combined with pork or beef, coarsely ground or in chunks; or a green chili stew made almost entirely of New Mexico green chilies.

Actually, the cultivation and preparation of fresh green chilies is a way of life in New Mexico. A few strains of green chilies indigenous to New Mexico have been coaxed, bred, cultivated, re-bred, and babied over the past several years to such an extent that the state now boasts several varieties whose flavors and heat levels are predictable. (They can't be absolutely predictable, given the fact that individual chilies vary so greatly in heat; two chilies on the same plant, for example, may have different levels of hotness.)

"There are five basic green chilies used in New Mexico at this time," according to Dr. Roy Nakayama, Professor Emeritus of Horticulture, New Mexico State University. "These are the New Mexico #6, the Big Jim Numex, the Scandia A, the jalapeño, and the Española Improved."

Dr. Nakayama, who spent 25 years studying and working with chilies, explained that "at least 80 percent of dried red peppers in use in New Mexico now are the New Mexico #6 which have been allowed to turn red and then been dried.

"The remaining 20 percent," he continued, "are either the Big Jim Numex, the Scandia A, the jalapeño, or the Española Improved. A few of these are allowed to ripen and then are dried. The New Mexico #6," he added, "is also used in Arizona."

The problem with fresh green chilies is that their skins are so tough that they must be removed before the chilies can be used in cooking. Most of us have to put our green chilies under the broiler or on the grill and blacken the skins before peeling and using. But in New Mexico markets, the chilies are roasted on the spot. When we visited New Mexico, we saw rotating drums do the job. JoAnn Mantych of Albuquerque described the process to us so vividly in a letter that we decided to include her account of the process:

"About this time of year (September) is chili time. People in New Mexico buy chili by the gunny sack. Yes, I said gunny sack, which is between 35 to 40 pounds of chilies. Families greater than two people often buy more. I am not kidding. Chilies are a way of life in New Mexico. The markets specializing in fresh chilies also provide roasting of the chilies, which is wonderful. For $3 or $4, they will put your chilies in a rotating drum of stretch metal and blast them with a propane flame. Then, they place your roasted chilies in a plastic sack for you to take home and peel. Their roasting process takes about 5 minutes. The smell of roasting chilies around these markets is absolutely mouth-watering.

"We take the chilies home immediately and peel them. Once roasted, the skin comes off quite easily. The skin is thrown away, the juices are saved for cooking, and most of the chilies are chopped and frozen in about 1-cup servings. The best and largest of the chilies are frozen whole to be used in chiles rellenos (chilies stuffed with cheese). Here, we seem to use chilies in just about everything.

"Many of the homes in New Mexico have *ristras* hanging by the front door, too. These are long strings of dried red chilies. When you need to make red chili sauce, you simply remove some chilies from the *ristra* and make the sauce from these chilies. The air is dry here and the chilies remain dry; mold is not a problem."

Note: Dr. Nakayama says that most *ristras* are made from New Mexico #6 dried chilies.

NEW MEXICO GREEN CHILI STEW (VEGETARIAN VERSION)

When we were served this dish in Santa Fe, the menu described it as a stew, but when we made it in the test kitchen, everyone began calling it a soup. Our feeling is that it is a kind of liquid vegetarian stew and that it should be eaten as a whole meal with warmed tortillas and butter. Made with fresh peppers, the stew has a slightly raw, delicious flavor—the perfect vehicle for fresh chili peppers. If you can use the fresh, substitute anywhere from 12 to 16 fresh peppers for the canned green chilies, and, of course, use any of the New Mexico varieties if possible. Otherwise, we think you will find this canned version excellent; it is soothing, easy to eat, and delicious. It is imperative that you use homemade chicken broth.

  3 **tablespoons vegetable oil**
  2 **onions, chopped fine**
  2 **cloves garlic, chopped fine**
  2 **fresh or canned jalapeño peppers, seeded and chopped fine**
  1 **large green bell pepper, chopped fine**
  7 **cups homemade chicken broth**
  4 **cups peeled Idaho potato, cut into ½-inch dice**

**6 4-ounce cans whole green chilies, hot or mild, seeds removed
   under running water, drained, and chopped coarse**
1 cup half-and-half, at room temperature

1. Heat oil in a soup kettle. Sauté onions, garlic, jalapeño peppers, and bell pepper for about 5 minutes over medium heat.

2. Add chicken broth and simmer for 20 minutes, uncovered. Then add potatoes and chilies and simmer another 25 minutes, or until the potato is tender.

3. Remove the kettle from heat and let sit for about 15 minutes, or until stew cools slightly. Measure; there should be about 8 cups of stew. If not, simmer it until the proper volume is reached. Allow to cool.

4. Stir in the half-and-half, mixing well. At serving time, reheat the stew but do not boil. If the stew boils, the half-and-half will curdle.

Makes 6 to 8 servings

ARIZONA CHILI CON CARNE

Arizona cooks use dried, not fresh chilies in their chili con carne, according to Judy Ratliff, food editor for the *Arizona Daily Star.* "The four fresh chilies most used in Arizona are Anaheim, jalapeño, serrano, and yellow wax chilies," she says. "But most Arizona cooks make their chili con carne in traditional Sonoran style using dried chilies, usually dried Anaheims, pasillas, and tepins. We soak them in water to soften, then we make them into a paste. We sauté chunks of beef, then simmer these in stock to cover until soft. We add only a tiny bit of onion, a tiny bit of garlic, perhaps a pinch or two of oregano to our Arizona Chili con Carne, which is a very pure dish. And we always serve our chili with a side of refried beans and with tortillas—sometimes with a side of rice as well. Arizona Chili con Carne is emphatically different from Texas Chili con Carne," she adds.

ARIZONA CHILI CON CARNE

- 3 **pounds round steak, all fat removed, cut into** $\frac{1}{2}$-**inch cubes**
- $\frac{1}{2}$ **cup flour**
- $\frac{1}{3}$ **cup vegetable oil**
- 5 **cups beef broth (good-quality canned broth is acceptable) or water**
- 6 **dried Anaheim chili pods**
- 6 **pasilla chili pods**
- 4–6 **dried tepin chilies, or more if desired**
- 5 **cups boiling water, or more if needed, to cover dried pods and chilies**
- $\frac{1}{2}$ **small onion**
- 2 **cloves garlic**
- 2 **pinches oregano**
- 1 **teaspoon salt**
- 8 **side dishes of refried beans**

Heated tortillas
Heated rice (optional)

1. Toss the round steak in a plastic bag with flour until the cubes are well coated on all sides. Heat the vegetable oil in the bottom of a soup kettle, then sauté beef until browned on all sides, stirring often with a wooden spoon to ensure that the meat does not burn. When the meat is browned, add the beef broth, cover, and simmer until tender, 40 to 60 minutes or up to 2 hours. Watch the level of the broth. If it goes down, add a little water or broth.

2. Meanwhile, place the Anaheim and pasilla chili pods in a bowl and cover with 4 cups boiling water. Then break the tepins in half, shake to extract their seeds, place the peppers in a small, separate bowl, and cover with 1 cup boiling water. Let the pods and peppers soak for an hour. (Do not soak pods and peppers together. When larger pods soak, their seeds leak out, and, since the tepin peppers are small, the two become difficult to separate.)

3. When the pods have softened, strain, reserving liquid. Remove stems and discard. Then hold the pods under running tap water to remove seeds. Place seedless pods in food processor or blender container along with onion, garlic, oregano, and 1 cup of the liquid. Process or blend until you get a paste.

4. Rub chili pod pulp through a strainer to extract skins. This will take only a minute. Add pulp to meat and stir well.

5. Meanwhile, strain the tepins and add tepin water to the other chili soaking liquid. Cut or tear up the tepins as small as possible and add them to the pot.

6. Add additional chili water to the pot, as much as needed for desired consistency. Arizona chili should be slightly thick.

7. Add salt, cook for a moment, and taste for seasoning. Serve each bowl of Arizona Chili con Carne with a side dish of refried beans and tortillas. Serve sides of rice also, if desired.

Makes 8 to 10 servings

VEGETARIAN CHILI

2 tablespoons oil

4 medium onions, chopped fine

3 large cloves garlic, chopped fine

4 fresh or canned jalapeño peppers, seeded and chopped fine

2 cups red and green bell peppers, chopped

3 1-pound cans tomatoes, with their liquid

6 cups water

1 6-ounce can tomato paste

3 medium zucchini, sliced in half lengthwise, then cut into thin widthwise slices

2 cups broccoli florets (all stems removed)

2 pounds mushrooms, washed, tips of stems removed, and quartered

10 tablespoons commercial (Texas style, if possible) chili powder

1¼ teaspoons salt

½ teaspoon each oregano and cumin

¼ teaspoon cayenne pepper, or to taste

1 10-ounce package frozen lima beans

1 10-ounce package frozen corn kernels

Warmed flour tortillas

1. Heat the oil in a large soup kettle. Sauté the onions, garlic, and jalapeño and bell peppers for a few minutes, or until the onion is limp. Add the tomatoes with their liquid, squeezing each tomato to break it up (or chopping it coarsely on a cutting board) before adding it to the kettle.

2. Add water, tomato paste, zucchini, broccoli, and mushrooms. Stir well and bring to a boil. Reduce heat to a simmer. Then add chili powder, salt, oregano, cumin, and cayenne pepper. Simmer for 25 minutes.

3. Add frozen lima beans and cook an additional 5 minutes. Then stir in corn kernels and cook another 5 minutes. Adjust seasonings and liquid content. Serve with warmed tortillas.

Makes 8 servings

HOSTING YOUR OWN CHILI CON CARNE COMPETITION

The first chili con carne contest ever held took place in Terlinqua, Texas, in 1967 and marked the beginning of a whole host of mock-serious events, both amateur and professional, throughout Texas and many parts of the Southwest. These contests were so much fun that they spread all over the country. If you're interested in hosting one of your own, here are some of the rules we worked out for our last competition.

Judges and Entrants

The competitions where 20 or more people compete are too complicated to hold at home. The ideal chili party, in our opinion, has six (and no more than eight) entrants and four judges. The judges can be the spouses of the entrants, but no entrants should also be judges. The host should not be a judge, although he may be an entrant. In addition you will need two "accountants" to add up scores and determine the winner and runner-up. All the accountants need to bring are calculators.

Other Guests

The party will be more successful if there is a small audience of people who are neither judges nor entrants with at least one neutral couple, who can be the accountants, if desired.

Instructions to Entrants

Tell entrants that they are each to bring a large pot of an *original* chili; winners and losers will feed the crowd after the competition. Chili should be transported in a large heating vessel, either a big pot, an electric frying pan, or a crock pot that can be plugged in. Entrants must be on time. A good time to start a party of this kind is 6:30 P.M. By 7 P.M. all entrants have arrived and judging can begin. Judging should be finished by 8 P.M. and the chilies can all be brought out for everybody to taste.

Helpers

You will need two kitchen helpers to assist you: the first to fill the bowls and put them on the tray along with the appropriate identification codes (see below); and a second helper to carry each tray to the judges and remove bowls when they are finished. Someone should begin heating the pots of chili as soon as the first guest arrives. The host will also need to have a list of ID codes on a piece of paper. As each pot of chili arrives, he assigns it an ID Code. (The host should write the name of the entrant next to his or her code. He should not attempt to remember them—he won't be able to do it.) Make sure that nobody but the host sees the codes.

ID Codes

Each tray that goes out to the judges must be marked. Before the party begins, figure out a code for each chili that will be coming in. If you have six entries, for example, the codes might be GH, ML, JK, QW, AR, BZ. Professional judges use random, double-letter codes to eliminate any prejudices associated with the highest or lowest letters. You will need to copy the codes onto the judging sheets (see below) and to write each code onto a large card. Each trayful of chili going out to the judges must include one of these cards so that the judges know which chili to judge on their judging sheets.

Judging Sheets

Make the judging sheets as simple as possible. Here is a suggested sheet:

CODES	SCORE	COMMENTS
GH		
ML		
JK		
QW		
AR		
BZ		

Have the judges score the chilies on a scale of 1 to 5, with the following values associated with each number: 1 = fair, 2 = good, 3 = very good, 4 = excellent, and 5 = superior. The judges should be asked to take into account the appearance, flavor, and aftertaste of each chili in making their decisions. No entry receives higher than a 5+.

Accountants

When all the chilies have been tasted and scored, collect all sheets and give them to the accountants, who will total the scores for each entry and announce the highest score and the runner-up.

Prizes

Prizes can be anything you want. We've had great success with such things as garlic presses, inexpensive bottles of wine, *ristras* (large wall hangings and wreaths made of dried chili peppers), garlic wreaths, bottles of champagne, etc. And, of course, you could give someone this book.

After the Judging

Once the judging is finished and the winners have been announced, bring out all the pots of chili (keep them hot during the judging) and set them on the table along with bowls, spoons, napkins, oyster crackers, French bread and butter, and any condiments, such as chopped onions, sour cream, guacamole, etc., that you like. After dinner you may wish to serve fresh fruit, but usually nobody is interested in anything other than coffee—everyone is too busy groaning in the corner from having eaten all the different chilies.

To Organize the Party

In the kitchen, you will need two helpers, six cards with an ID code written on each, a separate list of ID codes with room for the names of the entrants next to them, 24 clean bowls (use disposable if possible), and a tray large enough to hold four bowls, one for each judge. Besides this, it helps to have a judging sheet in the kitchen so you can see the order the chilies are listed in on the judging sheets. If you bring the chilies out in this order, it makes it easier for the judges; otherwise, someone invariably scores a chili in the wrong place.

In a separate corner of the kitchen, you'll need bowls, spoons, napkins, oyster crackers, French bread and butter, dishes of condiments, coffee cups, spoons, sugar, cream, and a bowl of fresh fruit for afterward.

On the judging table, you'll need two bottles of chilled, carbonated water, four glasses, 24 plastic spoons in two glasses (so judges can take a fresh spoon with each entry), a plateful of French bread torn into tiny pieces so judges can clear their palates between entries, four pencils (plus a few extra), and four judging sheets with codes already written on them.

In the living room, you'll need ice cubes, bottles of liquor (or just beer and wine), soft drinks, bottle openers, and an (optional) tray of cold appetizers. If you do serve appetizers, make sure they're cold and that you put them all out at once; you're not going to have time to fool with appetizers during the judging.

In the living room, you'll also need two accountants, two calculators, paper, pencils, and two hidden prizes. The rest is in your hands.

5
CASSEROLES

American casseroles, at least the most successful ones, have five layers, usually composed of leftovers. First, a starch, such as rice, potatoes, or pasta, forms the bottom layer and absorbs the juices that drip from the rest of the ingredients. Next comes a layer of cooked meat, such as beef, poultry, pork, or fish, cut into bite-size pieces. The third layer is usually some vegetable, such as tomatoes, corn, artichoke hearts, or peas. The fourth layer is usually a sauce, spooned over the top; and the fifth layer consists of grated cheese.

Southwestern casseroles usually follow the same plan. But they are not made with leftovers. Ingredients are prepared fresh for the casserole. Tortillas and tortilla chips, not rice or pasta, make up the starch layer. Because of their crisp texture, however, these will be more effective as the fourth layer from the bottom, rather than as the bottom layer. When the chips are higher up, then sprinkled with cheese, and baked, the finished casserole looks very dramatic—especially if it is then garnished with chopped jalapeño peppers before serving. It's also delicious.

To construct a Southwestern casserole along these lines, put anything—sauce, meat, or vegetables—as the bottom layer. The only thing to remember is that the meat goes over or under the sauce (or the vegetable, if it's especially moist) to keep it from drying out.

Meanwhile, here are a few tips on making Southwestern casseroles:

- ▶ Since Southwesterners usually cook the meat immediately before putting it into the casserole, you may wish to slightly undercook it at this step, since it will cook again when it goes in the oven.
- ▶ Never put a glass casserole under the broiler, not even for a moment. The heat will crack it.
- ▶ When smoothing or layering casserole ingredients, spoon them around the outside of the casserole. Never put ingredients in the center and push outward; it's much easier to cover the edges and spoon inward.
- ▶ When you are covering a casserole with tortilla chips, use fresh chips. They produce far better results than the commercial brands.
- ▶ Sauces that are too liquid will make whatever is on the bottom very soggy. If your sauce is too liquid, put it in a strainer over a pan and strain out some of the liquid. If you strain out too much, the pan will catch the excess and you can stir some back in. A drier sauce is preferable in a casserole.
- ▶ Most (not all) Southwestern casseroles can be made with commercial bottled sauces.
- ▶ When baking in glass casserole dishes, always lower the heat of your oven by 25°F, or watch the dish carefully. Foods cook more quickly in glass.

CHICKEN CASSEROLE WITH TORTILLA CHIPS

This delicious casserole makes a very impressive presentation.

Oil for deep frying
5 flour tortillas, quartered
1 recipe New Mexico–Style Green Enchilada Sauce (see Index), at room temperature
4 cups diced cooked chicken, at room temperature
1 cup sour half-and-half, at room temperature
1½–2 cups grated Longhorn cheddar
1–2 tablespoons chopped canned jalapeño pepper, seeded

1. To make the tortilla chips, first heat oil to 375°F. Fry the flour tortilla quarters on both sides, turning with tongs. Drain on paper towels.

2. Grease a 9″ × 13″ glass casserole. Spread Green Enchilada Sauce over the bottom to cover completely. Top with chicken pieces, as evenly as possible. Use a rubber spatula to cover chicken with sour half-and-half. Top with homemade Tortilla Chips, spreading them randomly, but covering the casserole completely. Sprinkle with grated cheddar.

3. Heat in a 350°F oven for 15–20 minutes or until cheese is melted and casserole is just heated through.

4. Remove from oven and sprinkle with chopped jalapeño peppers. Serve immediately.

Makes 6 to 8 servings

CHILE RELLENO CASSEROLE

This is a very delicious casserole that makes a dramatic presentation. Serve it for brunch, lunch, or dinner.

   8 eggs
   ¼ cup green onions (green part only), chopped fine
   1⅓ cups sour cream
   3 4-ounce cans whole green chilies, drained and seeded
   1½ cups grated Monterey Jack
   3 tablespoons jalapeño pepper, chopped fine
Oil for deep-fry
   5 7-inch flour tortillas, quartered
   1 recipe New Mexico–Style Green Enchilada Sauce (see Index), ladled into a strainer set over a saucepan and allowed to drain slightly
   1¾ cups grated Longhorn cheddar

   1. Beat the eggs with the green onions and sour cream until well mixed.
   2. Meanwhile, open canned chilies, rinse off seeds under running water, and spread flat on paper towels. Carefully pat to dry on both sides.
   3. Sprinkle ¾ cup Monterey Jack evenly over the bottom of a 9″ × 13″ glass casserole. Top this with half of the egg mixture, then arrange half of the green chilies over the eggs. Sprinkle 1 tablespoon of the chopped jalapeño peppers over the chilies.
   4. Repeat layers, sprinkling the remaining Monterey Jack, ladling the remaining egg mixture, and adding the remaining green chilies and one more tablespoon of chopped jalapeño peppers.
   5. Place in a 350°F oven for 25 minutes or until the eggs are just semi-set.
   6. Meanwhile, heat oil to 375°F and fry tortilla quarters, watching them carefully; use tongs to turn them until they're crisp and light golden brown on both sides. Drain on paper towels.

7. Remove casserole from oven when eggs are semi-set. Spoon Green Enchilada Sauce carefully over the eggs.

8. Top with tortilla chips, arranged randomly, but so that all of the casserole is covered with chips. Sprinkle the Longhorn cheddar evenly over the chips. Return the casserole to the oven for about 3 minutes or until the cheddar melts.

9. Remove the casserole from the oven. Quickly sprinkle the remaining tablespoon of chopped jalapeño peppers over the cheese and tortilla chips. Serve immediately.

Makes 6 to 8 servings

TEXAS CORN BREAD CASSEROLE

FILLING

- 2 tablespoons vegetable oil
- 1 onion, chopped fine
- 2 jalapeño peppers, fresh or canned, seeds removed, chopped fine
- 1 green or red bell pepper, chopped fine
- 1 pound ground round steak

CORN BREAD MIXTURE

- 1$\frac{3}{4}$ cups cornmeal
- 10 tablespoons flour
- 1 tablespoon baking powder
- 1 teaspoon salt
- $\frac{1}{2}$ teaspoon baking soda
- $\frac{1}{4}$ cup brown sugar
- 1$\frac{3}{4}$ cups plus 2 tablespoons buttermilk
- 2 eggs, well beaten
- 5 tablespoons melted margarine or butter
- 1 7-ounce can whole corn kernels, drained
- 2–3 cups Red Enchilada Sauce (see Index) or substitute a commercial sauce
- 8 ounces Monterey Jack or Longhorn cheddar

1. *Make filling:* Heat oil in medium saucepan and sauté the onion and jalapeño and bell peppers for a few moments or until limp. Add the ground round and cook, stirring with a wooden spoon, until the meat is well browned on all sides. Immediately transfer the mixture to a colander and drain off all fat and liquids.

2. *Make corn bread:* Mix cornmeal, flour, baking powder, salt, baking soda, and brown sugar in the large bowl of an electric mixer. Stir in the buttermilk, eggs, melted margarine, and whole corn kernels, mixing well.

3. Spoon half of the corn bread batter into a well-greased, 9″ × 13″ glass casserole dish. Spoon the onion and meat mixture over the corn bread batter. Spoon the enchilada sauce over this. Then sprinkle the cheese over the enchilada sauce. Spoon the remaining corn bread batter over the cheese.

4. Bake at 350°F for 45 minutes or until corn bread is lightly browned and appears done. Let the casserole sit at room temperature for a few minutes before cutting.

Makes 8 servings

WALKING TACO CASSEROLE

Our Walking Taco is served all over the Southwest, either as an appetizer dip surrounded by taco chips, or as a filling for warm tortillas. This recipe makes a large amount for a party. If you prefer, cut the recipe in half and layer it in an 8-inch square casserole.

- 2 tablespoons oil
- 1 cup onion, chopped fine
- 2 garlic cloves, chopped fine
- $1\frac{1}{2}$ pounds ground round steak
- 1 tablespoon pure ground chili powder, as spicy as you like
- $\frac{1}{2}$ teaspoon each salt and pepper
- 1 16-ounce can refried beans
- 2 4-ounce cans green chilies, drained
- 3 cups shredded Longhorn cheddar or Monterey Jack
- 2 cups Red Enchilada Sauce (see Index) or use a commercial substitute
- 12 scallions, green part only, chopped fine
- 1 $4\frac{1}{2}$-ounce can pitted black olives, sliced thin or chopped
- 2 cups Guacamole (see Index)
- 2 cups sour cream or sour half-and-half

Tortilla chips for dipping or heated tortillas for filling

1. Heat the oil in a large skillet and brown the onion and garlic. Add meat and brown on all sides. Then add chili powder, salt, pepper, refried beans, and green chilies. Mix well and allow to heat.

2. Spoon the mixture into a lightly greased, 9″ × 13″ glass casserole dish. Sprinkle cheese over the meat mixture. Spoon enchilada sauce over the cheese. Place in a 350°F oven for 20 minutes or until the casserole is heated and cheese has melted. Remove from oven and allow to cool slightly.

3. Sprinkle the chopped scallions and olives over the cheese, reserving a small amount to decorate the top. Spread the guacamole over the olives and scallions with a spatula, then cover guacamole with sour cream. Sprinkle reserved scallions and olives over the sour cream.

4. Serve at room temperature as a dip surrounded by tortilla chips, or warm as a filling for heated tortillas.

Makes a 9″ × 13″ casserole

BEEF AND CORN CHIP CASSEROLE

This recipe calls for commercial corn chips, which function as the starch in the recipe. Homemade tortilla chips may, of course, be used; but they will not improve the dish. Like so many Southwestern casseroles and dishes, this one uses a large amount of canned, commercial ingredients. Nevertheless, it is delicious.

> **4 cups commercial corn chips**
> **2 tablespoons oil**
> **1 onion, chopped**
> **2 large garlic cloves, chopped**
> **1 4-ounce can green chilies, drained**
> **1 pound ground round steak**
> **1 teaspoon salt**
> **2 cups Red Enchilada Sauce (see Index) or commercial substitute**
> **8 ounces grated cheddar**
> **1 4½-ounce can chopped black olives**
> **2–4 jalapeño peppers, fresh or canned, seeds removed, chopped fine**

1. Arrange corn chips in the bottom of a well-greased, 9″ × 13″ glass casserole. Meanwhile, heat oil in a large frying pan and sauté onion, garlic, and chilies for a few moments or until the onions are limp. Then add the ground round and salt, stirring often until the meat is well browned. When the meat is completely browned, spoon it into a colander to drain off excess fat.

2. Layer the meat over the corn chips. Spoon enchilada sauce over the meat and sprinkle cheddar cheese over the sauce. Top casserole with chopped black olives and jalapeño peppers.

3. Bake the casserole at 400°F for 15 to 20 minutes or until all ingredients have heated through and cheese has melted. Serve immediately.

Makes 4 servings

6

MEAT AND POULTRY

TEEN BURRITO BAR

Except for pizza, there's no type of food that teenagers like better than Southwestern. And we'd be hard pressed to find a meal that teens would like more than the burrito bar we're suggesting for your teenager's next party. We've assembled a basic menu consisting of three parts: two burritos—a fill-it-yourself bean and a fill-it-yourself chicken burrito—and a miniature version of our Southwest Sloppy Joe in a Bag (see Index), in which each guest gets his own ¾-ounce bag of corn chips, lays it flat on his plate (it should take up only about one-third of the plate), slits it open with scissors, then rolls back the edges to get a big scoop of Southwestern-style sloppy joe, which he mixes with the corn chips and eats right from the bag.

This party has been figured rather closely in terms of amount of food cooked. If you wish, add extra bowls of cheese and extra burritos and suggest cheese fillings to some of the insatiable eaters. Besides this, there will be extra sloppy joe mixture, which can also be used as a burrito filling. We are assuming eight teenagers.

For the party, you will need:

1. Sixteen 7-inch flour tortillas. (A 7-inch tortilla wrapped around a filling makes a burrito; a 10-inch tortilla wrapped around a filling makes a burro.)
2. A few 10-inch flour tortillas for the big appetites.

3. Three cups chicken filling for 8 burritos, a generous $1/3$-cup filling each (recipe follows), which can be made at least one day ahead of time.
4. Three cups bean filling for 8 burritos, a generous $1/3$-cup filling each (recipe follows), which can also be made at least one day ahead of time.
5. One recipe Southwest Sloppy Joe in a Bag (see Index), which can be made at least one day ahead of time.
6. Eight miniature bags ($3/4$ ounce each) corn chips.
7. Large bowls of each of the following: sour cream (or sour half-and-half); a double recipe of Guacamole (see Index); chopped lettuce; chopped fresh tomato; chopped jalapeño pepper, fresh or canned, seeds removed; chopped white or green onion; shredded Monterey Jack cheese; and chopped cheddar cheese.
8. Plenty of cold soft drinks.
9. A bowl of assorted fresh fruit.
10. A plate of Texas brownies.

At serving time, you will need to do the following:

1. Heat the bean filling, chicken filling, and sloppy joe mixture in three separate pots over low heat, making sure that they don't burn. The bean filling, especially, tends to burn quite easily.
2. Meanwhile, wrap the flour tortillas, eight to a package, in foil and place them in a 300°F oven (or wrap them in plastic wrap and heat them in a microwave oven).
3. Put tableware, plates, napkins, and glasses in stacks at one end of table. Place cold soft drinks (and an ice bucket, if possible) near the glasses. Set out several pairs of children's scissors (these are inexpensive at the dime store) and a tray filled with eight miniature bags of tortilla chips.
4. Transfer the heated bean filling, chicken filling, and sloppy joe mixture to large serving bowls with spoons. Bring them to the table immediately and place on a hot tray, if possible.
5. Wrap the heated tortillas (still in foil) in large kitchen towels or cloth napkins and bring them to the table.
6. Make sure your teenager knows how Southwest Sloppy Joe in a Bag should be eaten so he can show the others how to slit the bag and eat right from it. Make sure, too, that he knows how to eat a burro; this 10-inch flour tortilla is so big when it is wrapped around a filling that novices have trouble preventing leaks from the bottom end. One end of the burro should be folded up during the rolling procedure; eating starts from the opposite, open end.

7. Have fruit washed, dried, and arranged in a bowl. Have brownies or chocolate chip cookies (or both) already arranged on a serving platter. Keep the dessert in the kitchen until needed.

CHICKEN FILLING

This is the same filling as used in the chicken chimichangas recipe on pages 78–79, but here it's been doubled.

> ¼ **cup vegetable oil**
> 2 **onions, chopped fine**
> 2 **cloves garlic, chopped fine**
> 2 **16-ounce cans peeled tomatoes, drained and chopped coarse**
> ¼ **cup chopped canned green chilies, well drained**
> 2 **teaspoons pure ground chili powder**
> 1 **teaspoon each salt and cumin**
> 2 **heaping cups chopped chicken, white meat only**

1. Heat the oil in a heavy-bottomed frying pan. Sauté the onions and garlic for a few minutes. Then add the tomatoes and green chilies. Sauté for a minute or two.

2. Add the chili powder, salt, and cumin, and mix well to combine. Continue cooking, stirring often, until most of the liquid has evaporated and the mixture is dry. Remove the pan from the heat and add the chopped chicken. Mix well, transfer to storage container, and refrigerate.

Makes enough for 8 burritos

BEAN FILLING

$1/4$ **cup vegetable oil**
2 onions, chopped fine
2 cloves garlic, chopped fine
2 teaspoons each salt and pure ground chili powder
2 16-ounce cans pinto beans, drained
$2/3$ **cup milk**

1. Heat the oil in a heavy-bottomed frying pan. Sauté the onions and garlic over medium heat for a few minutes. Add the salt and chili powder. Lower the heat.

2. Meanwhile, place the beans and milk in a blender or food processor. Process until coarsely pureed. Spoon beans into frying pan with onions.

3. Sauté the beans, stirring constantly with a wooden spoon, making sure that the mixture does not burn. Continue cooking until the puree is dry, about 10 minutes. Transfer to storage container, allow to cool, and refrigerate.

Makes enough for 8 burritos

SOUTHWEST SLOPPY JOE IN A BAG

Sloppy Joe in a Bag is a popular meal with Southwestern teenagers. We think teenagers everywhere will enjoy slitting open a bag of corn chips, ladling in a big scoop of Southwestern-style sloppy joe (barbecued beef), mixing the corn chips with the sloppy joe, and eating the whole thing with a big spoon, right out of the bag. If desired, various condiments may be passed to be added to the bag.

   3 tablespoons vegetable oil
   1 large onion, chopped
   3 cloves garlic, minced
   1 green bell pepper, seeded, deveined, and chopped
   1 red bell pepper, seeded, deveined, and chopped
   2 pounds coarsely ground beef (chili con carne grind)
1½ tablespoons Gebhardt Eagle Brand or Fiesta Brand Fancy
       Light chili powder
   1 tablespoon ground cumin
   1 teaspoon chili caribe flakes
   ½ teaspoon each salt and crumbled oregano
   2 16-ounce cans whole tomatoes, with their liquid, chopped
   8 2½-ounce bags tortilla chips

   1. Heat the vegetable oil. Sauté the onion, garlic, and green and red peppers until almost tender.
   2. Mix in crumbled ground beef and spices. Continue cooking over medium heat for 5 to 7 minutes, stirring often.
   3. Mix in the tomatoes and simmer for 20 minutes, or until the liquid has evaporated.
   4. Adjust seasonings. You may want to add a can of tomato sauce for a richer flavor.
   5. To serve, cut a large *X* in the middle of each bag and turn back the edges of the cut. Arrange the bags on a serving tray. Pour the sloppy joe mixture into a serving dish with a ladle. Ask guests to take a bag of chips, ladle sloppy joe over the chips in the bag, and eat straight from the bag.

Makes 8 servings

Carne adovada (pickled meat) is the name given to a classic New Mexican dish in which meat (or fowl) is marinated in a paste made of ground onion, garlic, salt, spices, and a generous amount of any of the local chilies, coarsely ground. This coarsely ground chili is called chili caribe.

We've never tasted an adovada dish that wasn't great. So we're including two adovada recipes: one for the famous, traditional pork marinated in caribe and another for turkey marinated in caribe and roasted with corn bread stuffing, which you might want to serve at Thanksgiving or Christmas dinner. (See the New Mexico chili chart for sources of chili caribe.)

NEW MEXICO CARNE ADOVADA

6 pork chops, cut between ¹/₂ and ³/₄ inch thick
Adovada Marinade (recipe follows)

1. Trim off any excess fat, arrange the pork chops in a shallow dish, then ladle sauce on both sides. Cover and refrigerate overnight, 20 to 24 hours.

2. Brush off excess sauce and reserve. Arrange pork chops on prepared, oiled grill. Grill pork chops about 4 to 6 minutes on each side, 5 to 6 inches from ashen coals, or until all the pink is gone. The chops can also be placed on the top rack under the broiler and cooked on both sides until done. Cut into chops to test for doneness. Serve immediately.

Serves 6

ADOVADA MARINADE

1 **cup chili caribe flakes (any caribe made from New Mexico peppers will work)**
2 **cloves garlic**
1 **small onion, chopped**
1 **tablespoon sugar**
1 **teaspoon each dried, crumbled oregano; ground cumin; and cinnamon**
1 **teaspoon salt**
1½ **cups water**

1. Use a good processor fitted with the steel blade or a blender, and process all ingredients until smooth.
2. Pour sauce into a covered container and refrigerate until you are ready to use it.

Makes 1¾ cups

GRILLED FAJITAS

Fajitas are marinated, grilled skirt steaks served with guacamole, refried beans, sour cream, fried onions, barbecue sauce, and hot sauce in warm flour tortillas. The Spanish word for this cut of meat means "sashes." This dish makes a refreshing change of pace for the barbecue chef.

3 pounds skirt steak
Juice from 8 limes
1 recipe Barbecue Sauce (recipe follows)

1. Remove and discard outer flap or membrane from skirt steaks. Cut meat into 6 servings and arrange in a shallow dish.

2. Marinate meat $1\frac{1}{2}$ hours in lime juice, turning twice during this time.

3. While meat is marinating, prepare sauce and accompaniments.

4. Brush the meat with the barbecue sauce and grill both sides over ashen coals until cooked to taste. Because the meat tends to be thin, cooking time will be short. Fajitas can also be broiled 5 to 6 inches from the heat source or quickly fried in a hot cast-iron skillet with 2 tablespoons olive oil.

5. Cut cooked meat into $\frac{1}{2}$-inch strips, cutting against the grain, or serve whole.

6. Serve fajitas with guacamole, refried beans, sour cream, warm barbecue sauce, fried onions, hot sauce, and warm tortillas on the side. Or place fajitas in the center of a warm tortilla.

Makes 6 servings

BARBECUE SAUCE

4 tablespoons bacon drippings
1 large onion, minced
2 cloves garlic, minced
3 tablespoons dark brown sugar
2 tablespoons vinegar
$^3/_4$ cup beer
$^1/_2$ teaspoon salt
1 tablespoon Worcestershire sauce

1. Heat the bacon drippings in a heavy saucepan. Sauté the onion and garlic for 3 minutes, or until tender, stirring occasionally.

2. Add remaining ingredients and simmer for 15 minutes, stirring occasionally.

Makes about 1$^1/_4$ cups

SMOKED BABY BACK RIBS WITH BARBECUE SAUCE

A smoker makes a wonderful addition to backyard cooking.

6 pounds baby back ribs
Barbecue Sauce (see Index)

1. Cut ribs into portion sizes. Arrange in a shallow dish and marinate with barbecue sauce for 4 hours or overnight before smoking. Turn ribs during marinating.

2. Arrange charcoal briquettes in the smoker pan and start the fire. When coals are an ashen color, add twigs that have been soaked in water for 20 minutes. Use apple, plum, cherry, or other available fragrant twigs. (You can also smoke the ribs successfully without the twigs.) Place water pan filled with hot water in place in the smoker. Hot water speeds the smoking process.

3. Brush the ribs with barbecue sauce and arrange them in the center of the grill. Cover and smoke for about 2 to 3 hours, or according to the manufacturer's directions, and brush occasionally with additional sauce. We want to emphasize that the cooking time depends on how hot the fire is, how thick the ribs are, and how far from the fire they are. Serve ribs hot with additional warm barbecue sauce.

Makes 6 servings

GRILLED BUFFALO BURGERS WITH JALAPEÑO MUSTARD

This recipe can easily be doubled or tripled. The buffalo meat can be ordered from Wild Game, Inc. (see Appendix: Mail-Order Sources).

1 pound ground buffalo meat
1 small onion, chopped
Salt, pepper, and garlic powder to taste
4 jalapeño peppers, seeded, deveined, and minced
1 cup prepared mustard
1 cup Guacamole (see Index)

1. Mix ground buffalo meat with onion, salt, pepper, and garlic powder. Divide and form meat into four patties.

2. Grill the buffalo burgers, 5 to 6 inches from heat source over ashen coals. Use charcoal with some hickory chips, if desired. Use an oiled grill or an oiled grill basket, secured tightly. Grill burgers $1\frac{1}{2}$ minutes on each side, or to taste.

3. Blend jalapeño peppers and mustard in a bowl and serve with buffalo burgers. Pass guacamole and mustard at the table with the burgers.

Makes 4 servings

SMOKED BEEF BRISKET

Smokers are available in many large department stores and in hardware stores. Be creative about the fuel. In addition to charcoal, add a few twigs of apple or cherry, soaked in water for 20 minutes, or some mesquite.

1 3½–4½-pound brisket
Citrus Barbecue Sauce (recipe follows)
1 orange, sliced

1. Cover brisket with water in a large pan and simmer for about 2 hours. Drain.

2. Arrange the charcoal briquettes in smoker pan and start the fire. When the coals are an ashen color, add twigs. (You can also smoke successfully without the twigs.) Put water pan filled with hot water in place. Hot water speeds the smoking process.

3. Brush brisket with barbecue sauce and arrange in the center of the grill, topped with orange slices. Cover and smoke about 2 hours. Again we want to emphasize that the cooking time depends on how hot the fire is, how thick the meat is, and how far from the fire it is.

4. Check meat as it cooks and brush occasionally with sauce. Also check to see if additional charcoal should be added. Additional charcoal should never be injected with lighter fuel. Check manufacturer's directions.

5. When brisket has cooked, slice and serve with warm Citrus Barbecue Sauce.

Makes 8 servings

CITRUS BARBECUE SAUCE

The addition of citrus creates a tangy barbecue sauce.

2 tablespoons butter
4 green onions, minced
2 cloves garlic, minced
1 cup catsup
$\frac{1}{4}$ cup water
3 tablespoons cider vinegar
3 tablespoons freshly squeezed orange juice
3 tablespoons freshly squeezed lime juice
3 tablespoons light brown sugar
1 teaspoon Worcestershire sauce
$\frac{1}{2}$ teaspoon each salt and celery seed
$\frac{1}{4}$ teaspoon each Tabasco sauce and freshly ground black pepper
1 teaspoon Gebhardt Eagle Brand or Fiesta Brand Fancy Light
chili powder

1. Heat the butter in a small, heavy saucepan over medium heat. Sauté onions and garlic until tender, stirring occasionally. Mix in the remaining ingredients and simmer for 8 to 10 minutes, stirring occasionally.

2. Place cooled barbecue sauce in covered container and refrigerate until you are ready to use it.

Makes 1¾ cups

Only the Southwest—and particularly Arizona—has a humidity low enough and a temperature high enough to make possible a dish for which thin strips of beef (or venison or other meat) are hung out and dried in the open air. The sun-baked terrain of the Southwest did not yield food in abundance; a traveller or cowboy had to bring his own with him. The air-dried beef, called jerky, was nutritious, compact, and light. And it had a long saddle-bag life.

Besides this, it had a marvelous texture—chewy, when cut with the grain (which was how it was cut in the past), and tender with a slight brittleness, when cut against the grain. It was delicious, too. One jerky recipe, salvaged from the days when Arizona was a territory and reprinted in the *Arizona Territorial Cookbook* by Melissa Ruffner Weiner and Budge Ruffner, included a word of caution: "Whatever you do, never tell one soul what you are making. Jerky bums outnumber politicians in cleverness and sheer numbers."

The Mexicans and the Southwestern Indians all had their own versions of this dish before Americans took it over. The cuisine of the Sonora region, which has had such a strong influence on Arizona food, included several dishes using jerky in its shredded form. Shredded jerky is called carne machacada.

ARIZONA BEEF JERKY

3 pounds extra-lean bottom round, cut in $\frac{1}{8}$-inch-thick slices (ask your butcher to cut the meat for you, if possible)
$\frac{2}{3}$ cup lime juice
Garlic salt
Pure ground chili powder (picante)
Freshly ground black pepper

1. Put the meat in a large plastic bag, pour lime juice over meat so that juice touches all meat surfaces a few times. Place the bag in a large bowl, close it with a twister seal, and refrigerate for 6 hours or overnight, turning occasionally.

2. Next day, remove both oven racks from oven. Preheat oven to 150°F, using an oven thermometer. It is important that the heat be regulated and not rise higher than 200°F.

3. Cover one oven rack completely and tightly with aluminum foil and place it in the oven as close as possible to the bottom.

4. Remove the meat from the lime juice and sprinkle liberally on both sides with garlic salt, pure ground chili powder, and freshly ground black pepper.

5. Now hang each slice of seasoned meat over the metal bars of the second oven rack. The meat should resemble so many socks draped over a clothesline.

6. Insert the second rack in the oven so the meat can hang free, and let it dry out for 2 hours. Then pull out the rack and turn the meat strips. Cook another 2 hours, then turn the strips again. Do this two more times, for a total of four turns during 8 hours of cooking time.

7. Remove the jerky from the oven rack and lay it out to cool. When it is completely cool, slip it into a plastic bag, secure the bag with a twister seal, and refrigerate. Jerky will keep for a month in a closed plastic bag in the refrigerator. Eat as is whenever you want a low-calorie snack, or use in either of the following special recipes from Arizona (and Sonora).

Makes 1¼ pounds

ARIZONA BURRITOS FILLED WITH SHREDDED JERKY CON CHILE

6 large dried chili pods (see Arizona chili chart)
4 cups boiling water
4 large pieces jerky
1 large clove garlic
1 tablespoon margarine or butter
1 cooked potato, peeled and cubed
4 flour tortillas
Small bowls of chopped onion, chopped jalapeño, shredded
lettuce, shredded cheese, sour cream (or sour half-and-half),
and chopped tomatoes

1. Place the six dried chili pods in a large pot and cover with 4 cups boiling water. Let sit 1 hour. Remove chilies from water, reserving soaking water, discard stems, and run chilies under cold tap water to extract seeds. Set aside.

2. Meanwhile, place jerky pieces in a bowl and cover with boiling water. Set aside for 20 minutes. Then drain, and put them in a food processor or blender and process until shredded. Measure out 1 cup.

3. Place the peeled garlic clove plus 1 cup chili soaking water in the food processor along with the chilies. Blend as smooth as possible. Transfer the chili pulp to a strainer and rub it through with the back of a wooden spoon. This should take only a moment.

4. Heat the butter or margarine in medium frying pan. Add cubed potato and sauté for a moment. Add the shredded jerky, stir to heat, and add the strained chili. Simmer for a moment, then place over very low heat.

5. Put a clean frying pan over moderate heat to warm it. Place a flour tortilla in the heated frying pan for a few seconds to warm it. Then flip it over with your fingers and warm the other side. Repeat with the remaining three flour tortillas.

6. Transfer heated jerky and chili to a serving bowl. Serve with heated tortillas. Fill tortillas and sprinkle with condiments.

Makes 2 servings

ARIZONA EGGS SCRAMBLED WITH SHREDDED JERKY

2–3 pieces beef jerky
Boiling water to cover jerky
   3 tablespoons butter
   2 green onions, green part only, chopped fine
   3 eggs, well beaten
Salt and pepper to taste

   1. Place jerky pieces in a bowl and cover with boiling water. Let sit 20 minutes. Drain and process in a blender or food processor. Measure out $\frac{1}{2}$ cup shredded jerky.

   2. Melt the butter in a medium saucepan. Sauté the onions for a moment, then add the jerky to the pan and cook just long enough to heat through.

   3. Pour in the eggs and scramble over low heat. Add salt and pepper to taste. Serve immediately.

Makes 2 servings

HOMEMADE MOCK CHORIZO

Chorizo, a garlicky pork sausage, is used all over the Southwest and is also available in larger cities around the U.S. We feel that a homemade, mock chorizo is infinitely superior to the chorizo you can buy. So we're including a recipe for chorizo to be made two ways: one in which the mixture is formed into patties and fried; the other in which the mixture is sautéed all together while the cook breaks it up with a fork so that it can be sprinkled on dishes like Southwestern Pizza.

    1 **pound ground pork**
    2 **cloves garlic, chopped very fine**
    2 **tablespoons pure ground chili powder**
  $^1\!/_2$ **teaspoon each cumin and salt**
  $^3\!/_4$ **teaspoon oregano**
    1 **tablespoon each vinegar and water**
Oil or butter, depending on the method of preparation

METHOD 1:

  1. Put the ground pork in a large bowl. Add the garlic, chili powder, cumin, salt, oregano, vinegar, and water. Mix well to combine.

  2. Refrigerate for 4 hours to allow flavors to combine. Divide meat into five or six parts, form each into a patty, and fry in butter on each side until done. Drain on paper towels.

METHOD 2:

  1. Heat 2 tablespoons oil in a large skillet. Sauté the garlic for a moment, then add the pork, breaking it up very well as it cooks.

  2. Add the chili powder, cumin, salt, oregano, vinegar, and water to the meat. Continue cooking, stirring, and breaking up the meat until the chorizo is cooked through and can be sprinkled on pizza. Transfer to a colander to drain and cool.

Makes 1 pound

SCRAMBLED EGGS WITH CHORIZO

2 tablespoons vegetable oil
$\frac{1}{2}$ pound Homemade Mock Chorizo (see Index) or spicy sausage
1 medium onion, minced
1 Anaheim chili, seeded and chopped
6 eggs, lightly beaten
$\frac{1}{2}$ teaspoon salt
6 flour tortillas
2 avocadoes, peeled and sliced

1. Heat the vegetable oil in a medium skillet. Crumble the chorizo into the skillet.

2. Add the onion and chili, sauté until the onion is soft and the sausage is cooked, stirring occasionally. Pour off excess fat.

3. Add the eggs and salt to the sausage. Cook until the eggs are set, stirring lightly.

4. Serve hot with warm flour tortillas and avocado slices.

Makes 6 servings

PEPPER-SAUSAGE CORN BREAD STUFFING

    1 **recipe cooked Pepper-Corn Muffins (see Index)**
    ¼ **cup butter**
    1 **cup chopped celery**
    1 **large onion, chopped**
    ½ **pound chorizo or spicy sausage, cut into ½-inch pieces, casing removed and discarded**
 1½ **teaspoons rubbed sage**
    3 **cups crumbled or cubed day-old white bread**
1½–2 **cups chicken stock**

1. Crumble the corn muffins into a large mixing bowl. Set aside.

2. Melt butter in a large, heavy skillet over medium heat. Sauté the celery, onion, and sausage, stirring occasionally until the sausage is cooked and the vegetables are tender. Sprinkle with sage.

3. Toss the vegetable and sausage mixture with the corn muffin crumbs. Mix in the white-bread cubes and sprinkle with chicken stock, tossing lightly to mix well.

4. Place in a greased pan and bake for 35 minutes in a preheated 350°F oven. Serve hot.

Makes 8 to 10 servings

SOUTHWESTERN-STYLE MEAT LOAF

This dish is delicious served with Nacho Fries.

   2 **tablespoons oil**
   3 **large garlic cloves, minced fine**
   2 **small onions, chopped fine**
   4 **tablespoons finely chopped green onion (green part only)**
   4 **canned jalapeño peppers, seeded and chopped fine**
1½ **pounds ground round steak**
  ½ **pound ground lean pork**
  ¼ **cup pure ground chili powder**
   1 **cup flour tortilla crumbs (made in blender or food processor)**
  ½ **teaspoon each salt, cumin, and oregano**
   2 **eggs, well mixed**
   1 **8-ounce can tomato sauce**
   4 **whole chilies, canned or fresh (fresh chilies must be peeled)**
   4 **2-inch wedges cheddar or Monterey Jack**

1. Heat the oil in a medium skillet. Sauté the garlic, onions, green onion, and jalapeño peppers for a few moments, or until the onion is limp. Remove from heat and allow to cool slightly.

2. Meanwhile, put the round steak and pork in a large bowl. Add the chili powder, tortilla crumbs, salt, cumin, and oregano. Then add the onion mixture and mix well. Stir in the eggs and tomato sauce and mix well again.

3. Dry the canned chilies carefully. Insert a wedge of cheese into each chili.

4. Pack half the meat mixture into a well-greased, 9″ × 5″ bread pan or meat loaf pan. (If desired, line the bottom of the pan with a layer or two of parchment paper to facilitate removal.) Arrange the stuffed chilies on top of the meat. Pack the remaining meat over the chilies, pressing down to flatten the top.

5. Place in a 400°F oven for 15 minutes. Then lower heat to 350°F and continue baking for 30 to 35 minutes, or until well browned on the edges. Remove from oven and drain off fat. Invert onto platter. Serve immediately.

Makes 6 servings

ROAST TURKEY ADOVADA WITH BLUE CORN BREAD STUFFING

For an interesting and colorful variation, serve Roast Turkey Adovada with Blue Corn Bread Stuffing for your next party.

> 1 12–14-pound turkey, washed and patted dry
> Adovada Marinade (see Index)
> 1 medium onion, chopped
> 1 recipe Blue Corn Bread Stuffing (recipe follows)
> $\frac{1}{4}$ cup water
> Aluminum foil
> Meat thermometer

1. Remove all loose turkey parts, giblets, and neck; reserve for later use, as in a turkey soup. Cut complete leg portions from the body of partially thawed turkey. Place turkey and legs in a large shallow dish. Rub defrosted bird with Adovada Marinade. Cover lightly with aluminum foil, and refrigerate for 24 hours before roasting.

2. Sprinkle onion on the bottom of a roasting pan. Preheat the oven to 325°F. Spoon stuffing (see recipe that follows) loosely into turkey cavity or onto a greased baking dish. An alternative method of cooking the stuffing is to spoon it under the loose-fitting skin of the turkey breast. Pour water in the bottom of the roasting pan; transfer turkey and legs to the pan.

3. Cover the turkey with aluminum foil and roast, 20 minutes per pound, in the lower third of the oven, with a meat thermometer inserted in thickest portion of breast. Roast the turkey. One hour before you estimate the turkey will be done, remove foil and continue roasting. Check the thermometer. The breast portion will be cooked at 170°F and should be removed from the oven. Allow the legs to cook until they register 180°F on the meat thermometer. Let turkey and legs rest for 10 minutes before carving.

4. If the stuffing is to be cooked separately, place the dish in the oven 35 minutes before serving time. Slice the turkey, arrange it on a serving platter, and spoon the stuffing around it. Serve warm.

Makes 10 to 12 servings

BLUE CORN BREAD STUFFING

1 recipe cooked New Mexico Blue Corn Bread (see Index)

$\frac{1}{3}$ cup butter

1 large onion, chopped

$1\frac{1}{2}$ cups pine nuts

1 cup chicken stock

1. Crumble the blue corn bread into a large mixing bowl. Set aside.

2. Melt the butter in a skillet. Sauté the onion with the pine nuts until the onion is tender, stirring occasionally. Toss the onion and pine nuts with crumbled corn bread.

3. Sprinkle the corn bread mixture with chicken stock. Stuff the turkey according to recipe directions, or bake separately in a greased baking dish for 30 to 35 minutes at 350°F in a preheated oven.

Makes 8 servings

ARIZONA CHICKEN CHIMICHANGAS

Chimichangas are an Arizona creation and specialty, consisting of a flour tortilla rolled around a filling, either savory or sweet, and then deep-fried. Almost any well-seasoned filling can be used for a chimichanga. If you skip the deep-frying step and simply serve the flour tortilla wrapped around a filling, you are serving a burrito.

FILLING

2 tablespoons vegetable oil

1 onion, chopped fine

1 clove garlic, chopped fine

1 16-ounce can peeled tomatoes, well-drained and chopped coarse

2 tablespoons canned chili, well-drained and chopped fine

1 teaspoon pure ground chili powder (see Arizona chili chart for appropriate chilies)

$\frac{1}{2}$ teaspoon each salt and cumin

1 cup cooked chicken, shredded or chopped fine

$\frac{3}{4}$ cup each chopped fresh tomato and shredded Longhorn cheddar or Monterey Jack

12 7-inch flour tortillas

12 toothpicks (optional)

Oil for deep-frying

Bowls of any or all of the following condiments: guacamole, sour cream, chopped green or white onions, chopped tomatoes, shredded lettuce, grated Longhorn cheddar or Monterey Jack, red or green enchilada sauce, fresh salsa, and sliced or chopped olives

1. Heat the oil in medium frying pan. Sauté the onion and garlic over medium heat for a few minutes, or until the onion is limp. Then add chopped canned tomatoes, chopped canned chili, chili powder, salt, and cumin. Sauté this mixture over low heat, stirring often, until most of the liquid has evaporated and the mixture is dry.

2. Remove from heat and toss with the chicken. Set out 3 bowls for assembly: a bowl of chicken mixture, a bowl containing the chopped fresh tomato, and a third bowl containing the shredded Longhorn cheddar or Monterey Jack.

3. Set a heavy-bottomed, 10-inch skillet over moderate heat for a minute. Do not add oil. Lay one tortilla in the heated pan long enough to warm it well on one side. Then flip the tortilla over and warm the other side. When the tortilla is heated through, it will be pliable.

4. Spoon 2 tablespoons chicken filling in a band, 4 inches long, across the center of the tortilla. Sprinkle 1 tablespoon each of chopped fresh tomato and cheese over the chicken.

5. Fold the left and right sides of the tortilla up over the filling. Then roll up the tortilla until it resembles a cylinder. The filling should be securely enclosed. If you like, use a toothpick to hold the edge of the roll in place.

6. Repeat with the remaining 11 tortillas. Meanwhile, pour enough oil into a large, heavy-bottomed, high-sided skillet to measure at least 2 inches deep. Heat oil to 350°F on a deep-fat thermometer. With a slotted spoon or tongs, lower the chimichangas, one at a time (don't crowd the pan or you'll lower the oil temperature), and allow them to brown on one side. Turn them with tongs and allow them to brown on the other side.

7. Remove the chimichangas from oil and place them on paper towels to drain for a few seconds. Arrange on platter and serve immediately.

8. At the table, pass bowls of condiments to eat with the chimichangas.

Makes 12

7

VEGETABLES, GRAINS, AND OTHER SIDE DISHES

DOUBLE VEGETABLE PUREE

In this recipe, a pale green lima bean puree is served with a pale, burnt orange squash puree—an unusual and beautiful color combination that will please your eyes as well as your stomach.

LIMA BEAN PUREE

   2 cups fresh or defrosted frozen lima beans
$\frac{1}{4}$ cup butter, at room temperature
$\frac{1}{2}$ teaspoon salt
$\frac{1}{4}$ teaspoon each ground nutmeg and freshly ground black pepper

1. Arrange lima beans in a heavy saucepan and cover with boiling salted water. Continue cooking until beans are tender and still crisp, about 7 to 8 minutes. Drain.
2. Puree hot lima beans with butter, salt, nutmeg, and pepper.
3. Serve by arranging puree on a plate together with squash puree. A piping bag can be used for a more decorative effect.

SQUASH PUREE

   2 cups fresh or defrosted frozen squash
$\frac{1}{3}$ cup butter, at room temperature
$\frac{1}{4}$ teaspoon ground allspice
   3 tablespoons light brown sugar

Peel, seed, and cube the squash, if you are using fresh squash. Cook squash until tender and drain. Puree hot squash with butter, allspice, and sugar.

Makes 6 servings

SQUASH IN A PUMPKIN

We are adding a colorful tureen—a whole baby pumpkin—which is filled with chopped squash and spices.

> **6 small pumpkins**
> **6 cups squash or pumpkin, cut into 1-inch cubes, skin removed**
> **¼ cup firmly packed dark brown sugar**
> **1 teaspoon cinnamon**
> **¼ teaspoon ground ginger**
> **1 cup golden raisins**
> **1 cup chopped dates**

1. Cut a lid off the pumpkin, and remove the seeds and stringy parts. Blanch pumpkin and continue cooking for 5 minutes. Drain on paper towels and set aside. Preheat the oven to 325°F. Cook squash in salted water until almost fork tender, and drain.

2. Combine squash, sugar, cinnamon, ginger, raisins, and dates. Loosely fill the pumpkins with the squash mixture. Arrange the pumpkins on a cookie sheet and bake for 15 minutes, or until the pumpkin is soft enough to eat but not overcooked.

3. Place the pumpkins on individual serving dishes, and serve hot or at room temperature.

Makes 6 servings

BAKED CHORIZO IN A HALF SHELL

To prepare tortilla crumbs, tear stale tortillas into small pieces and crumble in a food processor or blender, 1 cup at a time. Store in a covered container. Add spices if desired. Kabocha squash grows in the Southwest. It is dark green and pumpkin shaped.

3 medium-size kabocha squash (or 3 large acorn squash), cut in half
3 tablespoons vegetable oil
1 large onion, minced
3 cups Homemade Mock Chorizo (see Index)
3 tomatoes, peeled and chopped
1 4-ounce can chopped green chilies, drained
1 cup beef stock (canned stock is acceptable)
½ cup chopped cilantro
1 cup tortilla crumbs
1 teaspoon ground cumin

1. Remove the seeds and stringy matter from the squash. Place the squash in boiling salted water. Reduce the heat to a simmer and continue cooking for 10 to 15 minutes, or until squash is fork tender. Drain and cool. Remove cooked squash from the shell, leaving outer shell intact with a ½-inch-thick wall. Drain squash upside down on paper towels. Mash remaining squash and reserve.

2. Heat oil in a large, heavy skillet. Sauté onion until tender. Mix in the remaining ingredients, except for the crumbs and cumin. Continue cooking until the chorizo is done, stirring often. Mix in the reserved squash.

3. Lightly fill the shells with this mixture. Season the tortilla crumbs with cumin and sprinkle them over the filled shells. Arrange the shells on a cookie sheet. Bake in a preheated 350°F oven for 5 to 7 minutes, or until hot. Serve immediately.

Makes 6 servings

PAN-FRIED SWEET CHAYOTE

Chayote is a light green, pear-shaped squash. It is available in many supermarkets and in Mexican grocery stores.

    1½ **pounds chayote squash, peeled and cut in half**
     4 **tablespoons butter**
    ¼ **cup firmly packed dark brown sugar**
    ½ **teaspoon cinnamon**
    ¼ **teaspoon each ground allspice and ginger**
    ½ **cup chopped walnuts**

1. Cut squash into ¾-inch cubes. Cover with salted water in a heavy saucepan. Bring to a boil, reduce heat, and continue cooking for 6 to 7 minutes or until almost tender. Drain.

2. Heat the butter in a skillet. Stir in the brown sugar, blend well. Continue stirring as the sugar melts. Add chayote squash, seasonings, and walnuts. Toss squash to coat as it warms. Serve hot.

Makes 6 servings

POSOLE

The word *posole* has two meanings. First of all, it refers to large corn kernels that have been treated with lime and then cooked. This is also known as hominy. When posole is not dried, it comes packed in liquid (both in its frozen and canned forms) and is used in making tamale dough and other dishes. For example, we have seen it pureed with cream, simmered with green chilies, mixed with cheese, and served as a vegetable.

Posole is also the name of a Mexican stew-type dish in which the lime-treated hominy is mixed with other ingredients such as chicken, garlic, chilies, etc., and then cooked until the kernels burst. When this happens, each kernel opens up like a flower, as in the following recipe. Posole (stew) is traditionally served on Christmas Eve and New Year's Eve in New Mexico. It can be served either as a side dish or as an entree.

POSOLE

Posole is traditionally served during the Christmas holiday, but it can be enjoyed at any other time of year as well.

$\frac{1}{4}$ **pound posole**
1 **medium onion, chopped**
1 **tablespoon chili caribe flakes**
2 **cloves garlic, minced**
2 **tablespoons ground cumin**
1 **tablespoon ground oregano**
2 **cups fresh tomatoes, peeled and chopped; or 1 16-ounce can peeled tomatoes, chopped**
$\frac{1}{2}$ **teaspoon salt**
$\frac{1}{4}$ **teaspoon freshly ground black pepper**
1 **pound oxtails, cut into 1-inch pieces**

1. Place all ingredients in a large, heavy saucepan. Cover with water.
2. Bring the mixture to a boil, reduce the heat to a simmer, and continue cooking. Cover for the first hour and then uncover.

3. Add water as needed, to cover only. Stir occasionally and adjust seasonings. The cooking time will be from $2\frac{1}{2}$ to $3\frac{1}{2}$ hours.

4. Serve posole hot in a deep bowl as a side dish or as an entree.

Makes 8 servings

CORN SOUP

Here is a beautiful corn soup, served with a whole ear of corn in each bowl.

> 4 **tablespoons butter**
> 1 **large onion, chopped**
> 1 **large red bell pepper, seeded, deveined and chopped**
> 1 **teaspoon chili caribe flakes**
> $3\frac{1}{2}$ **cups chicken stock**
> 1 **17-ounce can creamed corn, with its liquid**
> 1 **12-ounce can corn kernels, with their liquid**
> 6 **small ears fresh corn, husked**
> $\frac{1}{2}$ **teaspoon salt**
> $\frac{1}{4}$ **teaspoon white pepper**

1. Melt the butter in a large pan. Sauté the onion and pepper with the chili caribe flakes until the onion is tender, stirring occasionally, about 3 minutes.

2. Stir in the chicken stock, creamed corn, corn kernels, and ears of corn.

3. Continue cooking until the corn is just cooked and the soup is hot, about 5 minutes, turning the corn as necessary to cook. Season with salt and pepper.

4. Ladle soup into shallow bowls and place an ear of corn in each bowl. Serve hot.

Makes 6 servings

CHILES RELLENOS

Chiles Rellenos consists of peppers coated in a light batter, stuffed with cheese, and served with a heated salsa. They are also good stuffed with refried beans or leftover chili. Fresh chilies are best in this dish.

6 **mild fresh green chilies, poblano if possible**
8 **ounces Monterey Jack or Longhorn cheddar, cut into $\frac{1}{2}$-inch strips**
$\frac{1}{2}$ **cup all-purpose flour, plus additional flour for dusting chilies**
3 **eggs, separated**
$\frac{1}{2}$ **teaspoon salt**
$\frac{1}{2}$ **cup milk**
1 **cup vegetable oil**
1 **recipe Salsa (recipe follows)**

1. Roast and peel the peppers according to the instructions in Chapter 2 on pages 7–8. Cut a slit in the chilies and remove the seeds. Divide strips of cheese and place them in the chilies. Dust the chilies with flour and set aside.

2. Mix together the egg yolks, salt, milk, and $\frac{1}{2}$ cup flour until smooth. Beat egg whites until firm but not dry. Fold into egg yolk mixture. Let stand for 10 minutes.

3. Heat oil to 375°F in a heavy skillet. Roll the chilies in the batter. Slide them into the oil, cooking them two at a time until they are golden brown on all sides.

4. Place cooked chilies on a serving dish and top with heated salsa. Serve immediately.

Makes 6 servings

SALSA

- **2 tablespoons vegetable oil**
- **$\frac{1}{4}$ cup chopped green onions**
- **2 cups chopped tomatoes**
- **$\frac{1}{2}$ teaspoon each chili caribe flakes, garlic powder, and crumbled oregano**
- **$\frac{1}{4}$ teaspoon salt**
- **$\frac{1}{4}$ cup chopped cilantro or parsley**

Heat the oil and sauté onions until soft. Add remaining ingredients and cook for 4 to 5 minutes over low heat, stirring occasionally. Serve hot.

Makes about 2 cups

RED, BLACK, OR PINTO BEANS

A faster way of preparing beans is to first soak them overnight in 2 quarts of water and then drain before cooking, using fresh water to cook.

> 1 **pound dried red, black, or pinto beans, washed and carefully picked over**
> 2 **cloves garlic, minced**
> 1 **large onion, sliced thin**
> 4–6 **tablespoons lard or bacon drippings**
> ³/₄ **teaspoon salt**

1. Place the beans in a large, heavy saucepan and cover them with 3 inches of water. Stir in the garlic, onion, and bacon drippings. Cover the beans and simmer, stirring occasionally, until tender. Add water as necessary during cooking.

2. Different beans take different amounts of time to cook, but in general they are done when they are tender, yet firm to the bite, in about 2 to 3 hours. Add salt 20 minutes before the end of the cooking time. Cool beans before proceeding with recipes that require more cooking.

3. Cooked beans can be eaten straight out of the pot or used in preparing numerous bean-based dishes. Store cooked beans in the refrigerator until you are ready to use them. Beans will keep refrigerated for two to three days.

Makes 6 to 8 servings

REFRIED BEANS

Refried beans can be served with tortilla chips and garnished with a combination of chopped jalapeño peppers, crumbled goat cheese, and red or green salsa.

> 4 cups cooked beans, excess liquid drained and reserved
> 3 tablespoons bacon drippings
> 1 medium onion, chopped
> 2 cloves garlic, minced
> ½ teaspoon ground cumin
> ½ teaspoon each salt, freshly ground black pepper, and chili caribe flakes

1. Mash the beans with about 1 cup of the reserved liquid or enough liquid to soften them, using a masher or a food processor. Set aside.

2. Heat the bacon drippings in a large, heavy skillet. Sauté the onion and garlic until the onion is tender. Add mashed beans and seasonings, stirring continuously until the beans are of the desired thickness and somewhat dry. Add more cooking liquid as necessary.

3. Serve refried beans hot or at room temperature.

Makes 6 servings

REFRIED BEANS AND CHEESE

> ¼ cup lard or bacon drippings
> 4 to 5 cups Refried Beans (see Index)
> ¼ cup grated Longhorn cheddar or Monterey Jack

Heat lard or bacon drippings in a large, heavy skillet over medium heat. Stir in the beans and cheese and continue to cook over low heat, stirring often, until the beans have reheated and the cheese has melted. Serve hot.

Makes 6 servings

FAST REFRIED BEANS

Refried beans can easily be made into bean patties and fried until warm. Sprinkle with crumbled Mexican cheese or goat cheese.

   2 **16-ounce cans pinto beans, with their liquid**
4–5 **tablespoons bacon drippings or lard**
   3 **cloves garlic, minced**
   1 **medium onion, chopped**
 ½ **teaspoon each ground oregano, cumin, and salt**
 ¼ **teaspoon pepper**
Warm tortillas

1. Mash the beans in a blender or food processor, or use a masher, adding enough liquid to obtain the desired consistency. Set aside.

2. Heat the bacon drippings in a heavy skillet. Sauté the garlic and onion, stirring often, until the onion is tender.

3. Stir in the mashed beans and seasonings.

4. Continue cooking over medium heat for about 5 minutes.

5. Serve refried beans hot or at room temperature, with tortillas.

Makes 6 servings

SPANISH RICE

3 tablespoons vegetable oil or lard
2 cups raw rice
2 cloves garlic, minced
1 large tomato, seeded and chopped
1 medium onion, chopped
1 green or red bell pepper, seeded and chopped
1 fresh jalapeño pepper, seeded, deveined, and chopped (canned is acceptable)
$\frac{1}{2}$ teaspoon salt
$\frac{1}{4}$ teaspoon freshly ground black pepper
2 tablespoons tomato puree (canned is acceptable)
5–6 cups chicken stock (canned is acceptable)

1. Heat the vegetable oil in a skillet over medium heat. Add the rice and brown lightly, stirring often. Add the garlic, tomato, onion, bell pepper, and jalapeño pepper and fry until tender, stirring often. Stir in the seasonings and tomato puree. Mix in the chicken stock. Bring the mixture to a boil.

2. Cover, reduce heat to a simmer, and continue cooking for 15 to 20 minutes, or until all the liquid is absorbed. Stir the rice mixture occasionally. Serve hot.

Makes 6 to 8 servings

8

SALADS AND SAUCES

SOUTHWESTERN SALAD

This is the best salad we've ever tasted. To make it, you will need to prepare the Jalapeño Vinegar (see Index) the day before. All you do is buy fresh jalapeño peppers, cut off their stems, put them in a glass jar, and cover them with boiling vinegar. Although the vinegar gets stronger the longer it stands, it is ready to be used after 24 hours. The dressing uses the classic French vinaigrette proportions: one part vinegar to three parts oil.

DRESSING
- 2 tablespoons Jalapeño Vinegar (see Index)
- 6 tablespoons vegetable oil
- 1/2 teaspoon salt

SALAD
- 1 head lettuce, washed and torn into crisp pieces (see note)
- 1 firm tomato, cut into bite-size pieces
- 1/2 red bell pepper, seeded and cut into thin slices
- 2 green onions (green part only), chopped fine
- 1/2 cup each grated Monterey Jack, crumbled goat cheese, and black pitted olives
- 1/2 ripe avocado, cut into thin slices (optional)
- 2 fresh or canned jalapeño peppers, seeded and chopped
- 12 homemade tortilla chips (see Index)

1. Combine dressing ingredients and set aside.
2. Wash the lettuce well. Drain and dry it thoroughly. Arrange the lettuce in the bottom of a large salad bowl.
3. Sprinkle tomato pieces, bell pepper slices, and green onions over the lettuce.
4. Sprinkle Monterey Jack, goat cheese, and olives over the vegetables.
5. Arrange avocado slices on top of the salad and sprinkle everything with chopped jalapeño.
6. Mix the dressing well and toss the salad thoroughly to combine. Garnish each serving with homemade tortilla chips.

Note: Use the following method, if desired, to prepare each salad ingredient (except for the avocado, which will discolor, and the tomato, which will get limp) early in the day, combining them at the last minute for maximum freshness.

1. In the morning, wash the lettuce under cold, running water, meanwhile tearing it into bite-size pieces. Shake it thoroughly to get rid of as much water as possible. Then arrange lettuce pieces in a single layer on a long strip of paper towels. Roll up the towels tightly and put them in a plastic bag. Lettuce will have drained completely by dinnertime.

2. Chop all the other ingredients except the tomato and avocado and put each in a separate bag. Assemble right before serving.

Makes 4 servings

TOSSED GREENS WITH AVOCADO DRESSING

TOSSED GREENS

½ head romaine lettuce

1 small head Bibb lettuce

1 cup chopped walnuts

1. Wash and dry lettuce; crisp until ready to serve.

2. Toss greens with chopped nuts and arrange on chilled salad plates. Top with avocado dressing.

AVOCADO DRESSING

2 medium avocados

½ cup mayonnaise

½ pint commercial sour cream

2 tablespoons wine vinegar

½ teaspoon Worcestershire sauce

2 tablespoons freshly squeezed lime juice

4 tablespoons minced cilantro

2 green onions, minced

½ teaspoon salt

¼ teaspoon white pepper

1. Mash avocado pulp in a mixing bowl and blend with remaining ingredients.

2. For best results, use immediately. Dressing may be stored in a covered container and refrigerated for 1 hour.

Makes 6 servings

JICAMA STRIPS ON LETTUCE

Jicama is a root vegetable with the consistency of a raw potato and a crisp, refreshing taste.

1½ **pounds jicama**
Hot ground red pepper or ground ancho to taste
  3 **tablespoons freshly squeezed lime juice**
 ½ **cup mayonnaise**
  6 **small lettuce leaves**

1. Peel the jicama with a potato peeler and cut it into julienne strips. Place the strips in a deep bowl.

2. Toss the jicama strips with the red pepper, lime juice, and mayonnaise.

3. Arrange lettuce leaves on chilled salad plates and spoon jicama onto the lettuce. Serve immediately.

Makes 6 servings

GREEN TOMATO RELISH

Perfect for gift-giving time.

$\frac{1}{2}$ **cup light olive oil**
6 **cloves garlic, minced**
2 **cups chopped tomatoes**
3 **cups chopped green tomatoes**
1 **cup chopped and seeded red bell peppers**
1 **jalapeño pepper, seeded and minced**
$\frac{1}{2}$ **cup chopped cilantro**
2 **tablespoons Dijon mustard**
1 **cup white vinegar**
1$\frac{1}{2}$ **cups sugar**
1 **teaspoon chopped fresh dill**
2 **green onions, chopped, for garnish**

1. Mix all ingredients except green onions in a large, non-aluminum saucepan. Simmer over low heat, stirring often, until most of the liquid has evaporated and the vegetables are soft, about 1$\frac{1}{2}$ hours. The relish will have cooked down considerably.

2. Cool the relish. Place it in a covered container and refrigerate until chilled. Stir before serving and sprinkle with chopped green onions.

Makes 8 servings

GUACAMOLE

Store your guacamole with the avocado pits, which help to prevent rapid discoloration.

2 very large avocados, peeled and seeded
2 cloves garlic, minced
1 small onion, minced
¼ teaspoon salt, or to taste
¼ teaspoon pepper, or to taste
1 tablespoon olive oil
1 tablespoon lime juice
1 medium tomato, peeled, seeded, and chopped
¼ teaspoon cumin
1 canned or fresh jalapeño, seeded, deveined, and chopped

1. Mash avocados in a large bowl, blender, or food processor fitted with the steel blade.

2. Add the garlic, onion, salt, pepper, olive oil, lime juice, tomato, cumin, and jalapeño. Blend until almost smooth. The guacamole should be slightly chunky.

3. Place the guacamole in a covered container and refrigerate until serving time. Stir before serving. Discard pits.

Makes 2 cups

RED SALSA

Red salsa can be used as a dip for nachos and vegetables, or as a relish or sauce.

- 1 red bell pepper
- 1 jalapeño pepper
- 2 pounds ripe tomatoes
- 3 cloves garlic, minced
- 1 medium onion, minced
- 2 tablespoons minced cilantro
- $\frac{1}{4}$ teaspoon salt, or to taste

1. Seed, devein, and chop the peppers. Place in a deep bowl.
2. Remove tomato skins by blanching in boiling water for 30 seconds, or until skins are loose. Discard skins. Chop tomatoes and mix with the peppers.
3. Toss the first three ingredients in the bowl with the remaining four. Adjust seasonings.
4. Allow salsa to stand for 2 hours. Mix well before serving.

Makes 2½–3 cups

NEW MEXICO–STYLE GREEN ENCHILADA SAUCE

This typical New Mexico–style green enchilada sauce is much better if made with large, fresh green chilies. Since these are not usually available in most parts of the country, we suggest a canned substitute. If you can get large, fresh chilies (not green bell peppers), we urge you to use them.

2 tablespoons vegetable oil
1 medium onion, chopped fine
1 clove garlic
1 fresh or canned jalapeño pepper, seeds removed and chopped fine
3 4-ounce cans green chilies, drained, and chopped fine
1 cup half-and-half
$\frac{1}{4}$ teaspoon salt

Heat the oil, then add the onions, garlic, and jalapeño pepper, and sauté until the onion is limp. Add drained, canned chilies, half-and-half, and salt. Simmer for a few minutes, or until the sauce is thick.

Makes 2¾ cups

RED ENCHILADA SAUCE

1 medium onion, chopped
2 cloves garlic, minced
2 tablespoons olive oil
2½ pounds tomatoes, peeled, seeded, and chopped; or 2 16-ounce
   cans whole tomatoes, with their liquid, chopped
1 teaspoon any pure ground chili powder, or to taste
2 tablespoons cider vinegar
1 teaspoon basil
½ teaspoon each sugar and salt
   Freshly ground black pepper to taste

    1. Sauté onion and garlic in oil until the onion is tender, stirring often. Add remaining ingredients and simmer for 15 minutes, stirring occasionally.
    2. Adjust seasonings to taste. Cool the sauce. Place in a covered container and refrigerate until it is needed.

Makes 3½ cups

JALAPEÑO VINEGAR

Cut the stems off of the jalapeño peppers in order to release their pungency. Since the capsaicin, which causes the pungency, resides in the ribs and the placenta (the part enclosing the seeds) of the jalapeño, making just a single cut will spread the capsaicin all over the pepper and allow it to combine with the vinegar. The vinegar will be ready to use in 24 hours, but it will take a week before it reaches its full strength.

1 pound fresh jalapeño peppers, washed and stems cut off
1 clean glass jar (8-cup capacity), with stopper or lid
5 cups white vinegar

1. Put the jalapeño peppers in the glass jar. Bring the vinegar to a boil and pour it over the peppers. Let sit, uncovered, until vinegar cools.

2. Cover and refrigerate for a week. At the end of a week, strain and return the vinegar to the refrigerator, or store covered in a cupboard. Discarded jalapeños can be used in sauces or relishes.

Makes 5 cups

9
BREADS

SOPAIPILLAS

Sopaipillas are made and eaten all over the Southwest. But according to food writer Huntley Dent in *The Feast of Santa Fe*, sopaipillas belong to New Mexico. "In most instances," he says, "New Mexico's cuisine is a stepchild of Mexico's, but that is not true for these delightful little puffed breads which the state claims as its own." Note the similarity between these puffy little sofa pillows, as they are affectionately called, and Navajo Fry Bread.

NEW MEXICO SOPAIPILLAS

Sopaipillas are deep-fried, luscious puffs of crisp dough served warm with honey. They are used both as a bread and as a dessert.

    2 cups all-purpose flour
    1/4 teaspoon salt
    1 1/2 tablespoons baking powder
    4 tablespoons vegetable shortening
    3/4 cup water
    3 cups vegetable oil for deep-frying
    1/2 cup sugar
    Honey

1. In a deep bowl, combine the flour, salt, and baking powder. Mix in the shortening until blended. Add water and mix well. Turn dough out onto a lightly floured board. Knead dough until smooth, about 2 minutes. Roll the dough into a ball. Cover and refrigerate for 20 minutes. Cut dough in half, forming two balls.

2. Prepare one dough ball at a time. Roll first ball into a 12-inch square on a lightly floured board. Cut into 3-inch squares. Roll out remaining dough and cut into squares.

3. Heat oil to 375°F in a medium, high-sided skillet. Fry sopaipillas, two at a time, for 25 seconds on each side, or until golden brown. Remove sopaipillas with a slotted spoon. Drain on paper toweling. Sprinkle with sugar.

4. Serve warm or cool with honey.

Makes 32

BLUE CORN

Blue corn is not a dyed product. It grows naturally in the Southwest, just as yellow corn does. It is not unique to New Mexico; Arizona uses blue corn too, although not as much as New Mexico. In fact, New Mexico's fascination with blue corn has produced an interesting group of specialty dishes: the tortilla dishes such as blue corn tortilla chips and blue corn enchiladas, and blue corn corn bread dishes such as blue corn muffins, blue corn corn bread stuffing, and blue corn cornmeal battercakes.

The taste of blue cornmeal is bland. But the dishes it makes have a decidedly different flavor and texture from those made with yellow cornmeal. Blue corn is not just a different-colored substitute for yellow corn. It is a completely different ingredient and yields a variety of delightful dishes. The dark gray-blue color adds a unique touch to the dishes. A gray-blue tortilla, for instance, is visually more exciting than a yellow one.

NEW MEXICO BLUE CORN BREAD

This corn bread is often baked in a round layer cake pan or a cast-iron skillet.

$1\frac{1}{4}$ **cups each white flour and blue cornmeal**
$2\frac{1}{2}$ **teaspoons baking powder**
  1 **teaspoon salt**
 $\frac{1}{2}$ **teaspoon baking soda**
  3 **tablespoons brown sugar (optional)**
  1 **egg, beaten**
$1\frac{2}{3}$ **cups buttermilk**
 $\frac{1}{3}$ **cup melted butter**

1. Mix flour, cornmeal, baking powder, salt, baking soda, and sugar in the large bowl of an electric mixer. Stir in the egg, buttermilk, and melted butter, and mix well.

2. Spoon the batter into a well-greased, 9-inch square pan and bake in a 425°F oven for 30 to 40 minutes. When the corn bread looks done—it will have pulled away from the sides of the pan and will be slightly browned on top—give it 5 more minutes in the oven.

3. Let the corn bread sit for 5 minutes at room temperature. Serve it right from the baking pan, with or without butter.

Makes 6 servings

BLUE CORN TORTILLAS

Blue corn tortillas are not as pliable as flour tortillas, but have an interesting texture and taste.

2 cups all-purpose flour
2 cups blue cornmeal
1 teaspoon baking powder
4 tablespoons lard, at room temperature
1 cup hot water

1. Combine all-purpose flour, blue cornmeal, and baking powder. Cut in lard using a pastry knife, two knives, or a food processor fitted with a steel blade.

2. Stir in the water and mix until the dough holds its shape and can be formed into a ball.

3. Knead dough on a pastry cloth that has been very lightly floured, until smooth. (Kneading is not necessary if the dough has been prepared in a food processor.) Cover the dough with plastic wrap or aluminum foil and let it stand for 10 minutes. Divide the dough into 12 equal portions and shape these into balls. Again, cover the balls with plastic wrap or a damp cloth and let them rest for 5 minutes.

4. To form the tortillas, use a tortilla press or a rolling pin. First, pat the dough ball with your hands into a flat circular shape. Roll the dough into a 6-inch round on a pastry cloth, if you are using a rolling pin. If you are using a tortilla press, follow the manufacturer's directions.

5. Use a large, heavy, ungreased griddle or coated skillet. Very carefully place the tortilla on a medium-hot griddle. Fry about 45 seconds on each side, or until brown spots begin to form, turning the tortilla with tongs.

6. Arrange the tortillas on a plate and cover them with a damp towel if they are to be used soon. Tortillas can be covered with plastic wrap or sealed in plastic bags, and refrigerated or frozen. Reheat them on a griddle or covered with foil in a 325°F oven. Tortillas are best when used immediately.

Makes 12

NEW MEXICO STACKED
BLUE CORN ENCHILADAS

This characteristic New Mexico dish is made of three blue corn tortillas, stacked and layered with grated cheese, a sprinkling of raw chopped onion, and green (or often red) enchilada sauce. If you make the same dish, substituting yellow corn tortillas and red enchilada sauce, and top it with a fried, sunny-side-up egg, it becomes the dish that is a specialty of both Sonora and Arizona.

Hot oil for softening blue corn tortillas
12 blue corn tortillas (see Index)
 1 recipe New Mexico–Style Green Enchilada Sauce (see Index)
 1 pound Monterey Jack, grated
 3 tablespoons finely chopped onion

1. Pour the oil into a large frying pan to a depth of about 1 inch and heat to 350°F. Slip the tortillas, one at a time, into the hot oil for a few seconds till they soften. Remove and drain on paper towels.

2. You will be assembling four stacks of enchiladas (three tortillas to a stack). If you have four individual heatproof dishes, use them. Otherwise, use a large cookie sheet.

3. Arrange each enchilada stack as follows: one large spoonful of sauce, one tortilla, ¼ cup of sauce, 3 or 4 tablespoons grated Monterey Jack, 1 scant teaspoon onion. Place the second tortilla on top and repeat the layering with sauce, cheese, and onion. Cover with the third tortilla, but top it only with cheese, adding a little extra for the top. Repeat with the remaining three stacks, working as fast as possible to avoid sogginess.

4. Place in a 350°F oven for about 15 minutes, or until tortillas have just heated through. Serve immediately.

Makes 4 servings

NAVAJO FRY BREAD

Navajo Fry Bread, a deep-fried, flour-based bread, is made all over the Southwest, but its origins can be traced to the Spaniards who introduced wheat to the area. According to Navajo custom, the cook making the fry bread must poke a hole in the bread before frying it to let out the evil spirits. This hole also helps the dough puff up. You can use this bread as the base for Southwestern Pizza (see Index), or you can layer it with almost any kind of filling. We love it plain, served as a hot bread with almost any meal.

2 **cups all-purpose flour**
2 **teaspoons baking powder**
$\frac{1}{4}$ **teaspoon salt**
2 **tablespoons margarine or lard, softened**
$\frac{1}{2}$ **cup warm water (more if needed)**
Oil for deep-frying

1. Combine the flour, baking powder, and salt in a bowl. Stir in shortening, mixing well. If necessary, use your hands to combine the ingredients. Add warm water slowly and mix or knead again. The dough should form a ball and hold together enough to be rolled out easily. If you add the water slowly and judiciously, the dough will not stick.

2. Divide the ball into three parts. Roll each part into a small circle with a rolling pin. Do not use additional flour unless the dough sticks.

3. Now roll each small circle into a larger, 7- or 8-inch circle, or work the dough with your hands, pulling and easing the dough out until it forms an irregular circle, about 7 or 8 inches in diameter.

4. Heat the oil to 375°F. When the oil is ready for deep-frying, poke a hole in the center of each bread. Fry the breads one at a time, using tongs or a couple of forks to turn them so that they brown well on both sides. Drain on paper towels and serve immediately.

Makes 3 8-inch breads

FLOUR TORTILLAS

Flour tortillas are native to the Southwest and the northern area of Mexico. They are softer than corn tortillas and have a mild flavor.

3 cups all-purpose flour
$^1\!/_2$ teaspoon salt
$1^1\!/_2$ teaspoons baking powder
3 tablespoons lard
1 cup hot water

1. Combine the flour, salt, and baking powder. Cut in the lard, using a pastry knife, two knives, or a food processor fitted with the steel blade. Stir in the water and mix until the dough holds its shape and can be formed into a ball.

2. Knead the dough on a pastry cloth that has been very lightly floured, until the dough is smooth. Kneading is not necessary if the dough has been prepared in a food processor. Cover the dough with plastic wrap or aluminum foil and let it stand for 10 minutes.

3. Divide the dough into 12 equal portions and shape into balls. Again, cover the balls with plastic wrap or a damp cloth and let them rest for 5 minutes.

4. To form the tortilla, use a tortilla press or a rolling pin. First, pat the dough ball with your hands into a flat circular shape. Roll the dough into a 6-inch round on a pastry cloth, if you are using a rolling pin. You can use more dough and make larger tortillas. If you are using a tortilla press, follow the manufacturer's directions.

5. Use a large, heavy, ungreased griddle or coated skillet. Very carefully place the tortilla on a medium-hot griddle. Fry about 45 seconds on each side, or until brown spots begin to form, turning the tortilla with tongs.

6. Arrange the tortillas on a plate and cover them with a damp towel if they are to be used soon. Tortillas can be covered with plastic wrap or sealed in plastic bags, and refrigerated or frozen. Reheat them on a griddle or covered with foil in a 325°F oven. Tortillas are best when used immediately.

Makes 12

LARGE TORTILLA BASKET

Tortilla basket molds are available at many department stores and gourmet shops or can be ordered through The Chef's Catalog *(see Appendix: Mail-Order Sources). These large serving-size molds are popular for holding your favorite salad or meat combinations, or substitute potato basket fryers.*

1. Soften a flour tortilla in a hot skillet, turning it over quickly with tongs.

2. Fit the tortilla into the bottom half of the tortilla basket mold. Insert the top half of the basket gently and shut it securely.

3. In a deep, heavy saucepan, heat enough vegetable or peanut oil to cover the basket to 375°F. Lower the basket in the oil and fry only until golden brown. Remove from the oil and carefully release the tortilla basket from the mold. Drain on paper toweling. Add a favorite salad or meat filling, or fill with Nacho Fries (see Index).

PEPPER-CORN MUFFINS

1 cup all-purpose flour

1 cup stone-ground cornmeal

2 teaspoons baking powder

1 teaspoon baking soda

½ teaspoon salt

1 cup buttermilk

2 eggs, slightly beaten

¼ cup butter, melted and cooled

1 red bell pepper, seeded, deveined, and chopped

4 jalapeño peppers, seeded, deveined, and chopped

1. Mix together the dry ingredients in a large mixing bowl. Blend together the remaining ingredients in a separate bowl. Add the liquid mixture to the dry ingredients and just barely mix together.

2. Spoon the batter into a greased muffin tin, filling the cups two-thirds full. Bake in a preheated 425°F oven for 18 to 20 minutes, or until the muffins have risen and spring back when lightly touched. Cool on a wire rack.

Makes 12

PUMPKIN MUFFINS WITH GOAT CHEESE

    2 cups all-purpose flour
    $^3/_4$ cup sugar
    1 tablespoon baking powder
    $^1/_2$ teaspoon salt
    $^1/_2$ teaspoon cinnamon
    $^1/_4$ teaspoon ground nutmeg
    $^3/_4$ cup milk
    $^3/_4$ cup fresh or canned pumpkin puree
    $^1/_3$ cup butter, melted and cooled
    2 eggs, slightly beaten
    1 4-ounce package cream cheese or goat cheese, cut into 12 equal
      squares

　　1. Mix together the dry ingredients in a large mixing bowl. Blend together all the remaining ingredients except the cheese. Lightly mix in cheese squares.

　　2. Spoon the batter into a greased muffin tin, filling the cups two-thirds full. Bake in a preheated 400°F oven for 18 to 20 minutes, or until the muffins have risen and spring back when lightly touched. Cool on a wire rack.

Makes 12

10

DESSERTS

A WORD OF CAUTION

Do not use Mexican vanilla in the preparation of these or any desserts. We asked a spokesperson for the United States Department of Agriculture about Mexican vanilla, since it had recently been the subject of controversy, and she told us that Mexican vanilla definitely poses a health hazard. Apparently, much (but not all) of it contains a toxic substance called coumarin. Coumarin, a crystalline lactone, is found in many plants. It looks, tastes, and smells so much like vanilla that some vanilla growers use it to enhance the flavor of commercial vanilla. Consumers, however, cannot tell the difference between vanilla made solely from the vanilla bean and vanilla made from a combination of coumarin and the vanilla bean. Coumarin has been banned in the United States since 1954, because it can cause a variety of unpleasant reactions ranging from upset stomach to internal hemorrhaging.

THREE-DAY PECAN BOURBON CAKE

3 eggs, separated
1 cup golden raisins
¾ cup bourbon
¼ cup butter, at room temperature
1 cup firmly packed light brown sugar
1¾ cups all-purpose flour
1¼ teaspoons baking powder
¼ teaspoon salt
¾ teaspoon grated nutmeg
¼ teaspoon grated mace
2 cups chopped, shelled pecans
Cheesecloth
¼ cup bourbon

1. Twenty minutes before baking, separate the eggs, placing the whites in the large bowl of an electric mixer. Beat the egg whites until stiff peaks form. Transfer to a second bowl.

2. Place raisins in a shallow bowl. Sprinkle them with ¼ cup bourbon, reserving the remaining ½ cup bourbon for the cake batter.

3. Cream together the butter and brown sugar in the large bowl of an electric mixer. Add the egg yolks and continue beating until the mixture is light in color.

4. Sift the flour, baking powder, salt, and spices. Add the flour mixture alternately with the ½ cup bourbon to the butter, brown sugar, and egg yolks.

5. Mix in the raisins and any bourbon that has accumulated in the dish. Stir in the pecan pieces and fold in the egg whites.

6. Pour the batter into an 8-inch round pan with a removable bottom that has been greased, lightly floured, and fitted with greased parchment paper or brown paper.

7. Bake the cake in a preheated 325°F oven for 1 hour, 10 minutes, or until cake tests done, on a rack set in the lower third of the oven. Allow the cake to cool 10 minutes in the pan. Remove and place on a wire rack to cool.

8. Soak the cheesecloth in the remaining ¼ cup bourbon. Wrap the cake in the cheesecloth and let it stand in a dry place or in a cake tin for three days.

9. Cut in small slices. Serve with sweetened whipped cream, if desired.

Makes 8 servings

CHOCOLATE CAKE WITH PRUNES

  2 **ounces unsweetened chocolate**
  6 **tablespoons butter**
  ³/₄ **cup sugar**
  2 **eggs**
  1¹/₂ **cups all-purpose flour**
  1¹/₄ **teaspoons baking powder**
  ¹/₄ **teaspoon each baking soda and salt**
  ¹/₂ **cup milk mixed with 1¹/₂ teaspoons lemon juice**
  1 **teaspoon vanilla**
  1¹/₄ **cups pitted, stewed, chopped prunes**

1. Melt the chocolate in the top of a double boiler over simmering water, or in a microwave oven. Cool and set aside.

2. Mix the butter and sugar together until blended and light.

3. Add the eggs, one at a time, and beat well after each addition. Mix in the chocolate.

4. Sift the flour, baking powder, baking soda, and salt together.

5. Add the dry ingredients alternately with the sour milk to the first mixture.

6. Stir in the vanilla and chopped prunes.

7. Spoon the batter into a greased and lightly floured 9-inch decorative ring mold and bake in a preheated 375°F oven for 40 minutes, or until the cake springs back when lightly touched. Invert the cake onto a wire rack and cool.

8. Glaze the cake or sprinkle with confectioners' sugar, if desired.

CHOCOLATE GLAZE

  6 **ounces semisweet chocolate**
  2 **tablespoons butter**

Melt the chocolate and butter in the top of a double boiler over simmering water. Stir until the mixture is well blended. Cool for 5 minutes and drizzle over cooled cake.

Makes 8 servings

TUCSON LEMON CASSEROLE CAKE

Lemon cakes are very popular in Arizona. This one is served in many Tucson homes.

CAKE

$^3/_4$ **cup butter**

1$^2/_3$ **cups sugar**

2$^1/_2$ **teaspoons baking powder**

$^1/_2$ **teaspoon salt**

2 **tablespoons lemon rind, grated fine**

3 **eggs**

2$^1/_2$ **cups flour, sifted before measuring**

1 **cup milk**

2 **tablespoons fresh, strained lemon juice**

LEMON GLAZE

10 **tablespoons fresh, strained lemon juice**

1$^1/_3$ **cups confectioners' sugar**

1. Cream butter with sugar until fluffy. Beat in baking powder, salt, and lemon rind.

2. Beat in eggs, one at a time. Then add flour alternately with milk, beginning and ending with flour. Add 2 tablespoons lemon juice and beat until well combined.

3. Spoon this batter into a greased and floured 9″ × 13″ glass casserole dish and bake in a 350°F oven for 30 to 40 minutes or until the cake has pulled away from the sides and looks lightly browned on top.

4. Meanwhile, mix the 10 tablespoons lemon juice with the confectioners' sugar and allow the mixture to sit, stirring occasionally while the cake bakes.

5. When the cake is done, allow it to cool in the pan for 3 to 4 minutes, then invert onto a wire rack.

6. Immediately begin making tiny "gopher" holes in the top of the cake with a $^1/_4$-inch-thick stick, the kind used for taffy apples. Spoon a teaspoon or so of the glaze down every hole. Continue making holes until the whole surface of the cake is covered. Then brush and spoon the remaining glaze over the top of the cake to cover. Allow to cool.

Makes a 9″ × 13″ cake

PECAN UPSIDE-DOWN CAKE

This version of the upside-down cake is prepared in a skillet.

TOPPING

$^1/_4$ **cup butter**

$^2/_3$ **cup firmly packed dark brown sugar**

2 **cups pecan halves**

BATTER

$1^1/_4$ **cups all-purpose flour**

$1^1/_2$ **teaspoons baking powder**

$^1/_4$ **teaspoon salt**

1 **cup sugar**

2 **egg yolks, well beaten**

$^3/_4$ **cup milk**

1 **teaspoon vanilla**

2 **egg whites, stiffly beaten**

1. Melt the butter in a 9-inch heavy skillet suitable for use in the oven. Stir in the sugar until it is evenly distributed. Sprinkle the pecans evenly over the sugar. Set the skillet aside. Prepare cake batter.

2. Sift the flour, baking powder, and salt, and set aside.

3. Blend the sugar into the well-beaten egg yolks until the mixture is light in color. Add the milk and vanilla and stir.

4. Add the dry ingredients to the sugar, egg yolks, and milk.

5. Fold in the stiffly beaten egg whites.

6. Carefully ladle the batter over the pecan topping.

7. Bake in a preheated 350°F oven for 50 minutes, or until the cake springs back when lightly touched. Loosen around the sides with a knife. Cover the cake with a plate or tray and carefully turn it upside down. Let the cake stand 2 minutes before removing the skillet. Cool the cake before serving.

Makes 6 to 8 servings

NOGALES LEMON CAKE

1 cup butter, at room temperature, cut into ½-inch pieces
2 cups sugar
3 eggs
3 cups cake flour
½ teaspoon baking soda
1 cup buttermilk
3 tablespoons lemon zest
3½ tablespoons freshly squeezed lemon juice
½ cup chopped walnuts

1. Cream the butter in the large bowl of an electric mixer until it is light and fluffy. Stir in the sugar slowly and continue mixing until the mixture is light in color.

2. Add the eggs, one at a time, and beat until they are incorporated.

3. Sift flour and baking soda into a bowl. Stir the flour into the batter alternately with the buttermilk, stirring only until batter is smooth.

4. Mix in the lemon zest, lemon juice, and half of the walnuts. Reserve the remaining nuts for topping.

5. Pour the batter into a greased and floured, 9-inch tube pan with removable bottom or 12-cup bundt pan. Bake in a preheated 325°F oven on a rack in the lower third of the oven for 1 hour, 10 minutes, or until the cake tests done. While the cake is baking, prepare the icing.

LEMON ICING

½ cup butter, at room temperature, cut into ½-inch pieces
2 cups confectioners' sugar, sifted
2 tablespoons lemon zest
6 tablespoons freshly squeezed lemon juice

1. Cream the butter in the large bowl of an electric mixer with the confectioners' sugar. Mix in the zest and lemon juice. The icing should be of spreading consistency.

2. Allow the cake to stand for 4 or 5 minutes in the pan. Remove the cake from the pan and place it on a wire rack over a cookie sheet. Prick the cake repeatedly with a long toothpick. Spread the glaze over the top and sides of the hot cake. Continue glazing until all the icing is used. Scatter the remaining walnuts decoratively over the top of the cake. Cool cake completely before serving.

Makes 10 to 12 servings

INDIVIDUAL COFFEE FLANS

$^3/_4$ **cup sugar**
3 **tablespoons water**
5 **eggs**
1 **12-ounce can evaporated milk**
$1^1/_2$ **tablespoons instant coffee**
1 **cup water**
$^3/_4$ **cup sugar**
$1^1/_2$ **teaspoons vanilla**

1. Melt the sugar and the 3 tablespoons water in a small, heavy saucepan until the syrup is golden brown, stirring often. Pour melted sugar syrup into the bottom of six or eight individual $^1/_2$-cup molds, turning and tipping the molds to coat bottom and sides. Arrange the molds on a cookie sheet, and refrigerate until you are ready to use them and syrup has hardened.

2. Preheat the oven to 350°F. Fill a shallow pan that is large enough to hold all the molds with 1 inch of hot water.

3. Beat the eggs until light and mix in the evaporated milk. Dissolve the instant coffee in water and add it to the egg mixture. Stir in the sugar and vanilla.

4. Pour the flan into the prepared molds and set them in the prepared pan.

5. Bake for 50 minutes, or until the custard is set. A knife inserted into the custard will come out clean when it is done. Cool. Loosen the edges of the mold with a sharp knife and unmold onto individual serving dishes. Serve cold.

Makes 6 to 8 servings

FLAN IN A RING MOLD

If vanilla beans are not readily available, substitute 1½ teaspoons vanilla extract and add it to the cooled milk. Flan can be served with sliced fruit or frosted grapes.

1 **cup sugar**
3 **tablespoons water**
5 **cups milk**
1 **vanilla bean, slit**
6 **eggs**

1. Heat ½ cup sugar and water in a small, heavy saucepan. Cook over medium heat, stirring until the sugar melts and forms a light brown syrup. Pour the syrup into a 6-cup ring mold. Tip the mold from side to side to coat the entire bottom of the pan with syrup. Refrigerate pan until needed.

2. Heat the milk and vanilla bean until the milk comes to a boil over medium heat. Discard the vanilla bean. Cool milk.

3. Beat the eggs and remaining ½ cup sugar in the large bowl of an electric mixer until smooth.

4. Pour the custard into the prepared mold. Fill a shallow pan that is larger than the mold with 1½ inches of water. Place the pan in a preheated 350°F oven. Add the mold to the pan. Bake 50 to 60 minutes or until the flan has set. It will be firm to the touch and a knife inserted in the center will come out clean.

5. Cool the custard and refrigerate for 3 hours. Loosen the sides of the custard and unmold onto a serving plate.

Makes 6 to 8 servings

ALMOND WEDDING COOKIES

1 cup butter, at room temperature, cut into small pieces
¾ cup confectioners' sugar
1 teaspoon vanilla
2 cups all-purpose flour, sifted
½ teaspoon cream of tartar
1 cup chopped almonds
Confectioners' sugar

1. Cream the butter, sugar, and vanilla in the large bowl of an electric mixer.
2. Mix in the flour and cream of tartar. Blend in the almonds by hand. Place the dough in a covered container and chill for 30 minutes.
3. Form the dough into ¾-inch walnut-size balls and arrange on an ungreased cookie sheet.
4. Bake in a preheated 325°F oven for 15 to 20 minutes. The cookies should retain their shape.
5. Remove the cookies from the cookie sheet while they are still hot and roll them in the confectioners' sugar. Place the cookies on a dish and cool.
6. Roll them again in sugar. Serve cold. Almond wedding cookies can be stored in a covered container.

Makes 40

DATEBARS IN A CORNMEAL CRUST

CRUST

1½ cups flour for crust, plus ½ cup for the top crust

⅔ cup cornmeal

6 tablespoons brown sugar

¾ teaspoon baking soda

6 tablespoons butter, softened

1 egg

¼ cup water

FILLING

1 pound pitted dates

1½ cups water

1 cup brown sugar

2 teaspoons vanilla

1. Combine 1½ cups flour, ⅔ cup cornmeal, 6 tablespoons brown sugar, and the baking soda in a bowl and mix well to combine. Stir in the butter or use your hands to combine. Stir in the egg and ¼ cup water. Knead for a moment.

2. Take two-thirds of this mixture and pat it into the bottom of a 9″ × 13″ glass casserole. Place in a 350°F oven for 30 minutes or until the crust is cooked through but not completely browned.

3. Sprinkle the remaining ½ cup flour over the remaining third of the cornmeal mixture. Knead for a moment; the mixture should begin to fall apart like streusel. If it does not, add small pinches of flour until it does.

4. Meanwhile, put the dates, water, and 1 cup brown sugar in a small, heavy-bottomed saucepan and bring to a boil. Reduce heat to medium and cook, stirring occasionally, until mixture is soft and thick, about 20 minutes.

5. Allow to cool slightly, then stir in vanilla.

6. Spoon the date mixture over the crust carefully. Sprinkle the cornmeal "streusel" on top of the date mixture. Topping will be thick.

7. Bake in a 350°F oven for 30 to 40 minutes or until the topping is brown on the edges and top.

8. Remove from the oven and set on a wire rack to cool. Cut into squares.

Makes a 9″ × 13″ casserole

RED GRAPEFRUIT SORBET

8 medium Texas Ruby Red grapefruits, cut in half
Red grapefruit juice
1 cup sugar
2 cups water
1 egg white, at room temperature
8 lettuce leaves, red if available, for garnish

1. Section the grapefruit and puree. Place the puree in a shallow bowl. Freeze the grapefruit shells to use as serving cups.

2. Add enough red grapefruit juice to the puree to make 2 cups total. Set aside.

3. Heat the sugar and water over medium heat until they reach 230°F on a candy thermometer. Cool. Mix the syrup with the grapefruit puree, and freeze in a shallow tray. When the mixture is frozen, spoon it into a food processor fitted with the steel blade and process it until it becomes slushy.

4. Beat the egg white until firm peaks form. Fold it into the slush and refreeze. When you are ready to serve, arrange a lettuce leaf decoratively in each frozen grapefruit shell. Scoop or spoon sorbet onto the lettuce leaf. Serve immediately.

Makes 8 servings

GUAVA SLUSH

The alcohol will prevent the guava slush from turning to ice.

3 **12-ounce cans guava nectar**
4 **ounces tequila**
1 **cup sweetened whipped cream**
2 **cups sliced strawberries**

1. Combine the guava nectar and tequila in a shallow bowl or tray. Cover and freeze until firm.

2. Spoon the guava slush into sherbet dishes or ice cream cones.

3. Garnish with sweetened whipped cream and sliced strawberries.

Makes 6 servings

11
QUICK AND EASY DISHES

In a hurry?

The following suggestions take less than 10 minutes to prepare, for those days when something simple yet delicious is called for. Experiment with these popular dishes:

1. For a chili-cheese omelet, add 2 ounces drained and chopped, canned mild peppers and 3 to 5 ounces grated Longhorn cheddar or Monterey Jack to your favorite omelet recipe. Serve garnished with sour cream and chopped cilantro.

2. Add chopped tomatoes, fried chopped onions and garlic, and hot pepper to taste to canned chili. A teaspoon of Gebhardt Eagle Brand or Fiesta Brand Fancy Light chili powder will do wonders.

3. Canned beans can be partially drained, mashed, and then fried over medium heat in bacon drippings with chopped onions and garlic for a fast rendition of refried beans.

4. For dessert, try fresh figs, goat cheese, and crackers.

5. Sprinkle skinned chicken breasts thickly with pure ground chili powder before grilling or broiling.

You can find these other tasty 10-minute dishes throughout *The Southwestern Sampler*. Just look up your choice in the Index:

Scrambled Eggs with Chorizo
Jicama Strips on Lettuce
Blue Corn Nachos
Fast Refried Beans
Gringo Tostadas

APPENDIX: MAIL-ORDER SOURCES

Blue Mesa Restaurant (and Grocery Store)
1729 North Halsted
Chicago, Illinois 60614

Bolner's Fiesta Products
426 Menchaca
San Antonio, Texas 78207

Buenos Foods
P.O. Box 293
Albuquerque, New Mexico 87103

Casados Farms
P.O. Box 1269
San Juan Pueblo, New Mexico 87566

The Chef's Catalog
3215 Commercial Avenue
Northbrook, Illinois 60062
(Tortilla basket fryer)

Dean and Deluca
Mail Order Department
110 Greene Street, Suite 304
New York, New York 10012

La Preferida, Inc.
3400 West 35th Street
Chicago, Illinois 60632

Lazy Susan, Inc.
P.O. Box 10438
1702 South Presa
San Antonio, Texas 78210

Maid of Scandinavia
3244 Raleigh Avenue
Minneapolis, Minnesota 55416

Mexican Connection from Old Santa Fe
142 Lincoln Avenue
Santa Fe, New Mexico 87501

Monterrey Food Products
3939 Brooklyn Avenue
Los Angeles, California 90063-1899

Morgan's
Mexican-Lebanese Foods
726 South Robert Street
St. Paul, Minnesota 55107

Old El Paso
P.O. Box 392
St. Louis, Missouri 63166

Reynoso Bros. Foods Corp.
2025 South Central
Los Angeles, California 90011

Ross's Blue Heaven Blue Corn Chips
8812 4th Street Northwest
Albuquerque, New Mexico
(Blue corn chips, blue corn muffin mix, blue
corn pancake mix)

Sey-Co Products Co., Inc.
7651 Densmore Avenue
Van Nuys, California 91406

South Texas Spice Company, Inc.
P.O. Box 680086
San Antonio, Texas 78268

Wild Game, Inc.
1941 West Division Street
Chicago, Illinois 60022

INDEX